HEAR THE MESSAGES FROM BEYOND THROUGH MEDIUMSHIP

There has been a revival of spiritualism in recent years, with more and more people attempting to communicate with disembodied spirits via talking boards, séances, and all forms of mediumship (such as allowing another spirit to make use of your vocal chords, hand muscles, etc., while you remain in control of your body). The movement, which began in 1848 with the Fox sisters of New York, has attracted the likes of Abraham Lincoln and Queen Victoria, and even blossomed into a full-scale religion with regular services of hymns, prayers, Bible-reading and sermons along with spirit communication.

Doors to Other Worlds is for *anyone* who wishes to communicate with spirits, as well as for the less adventurous who simply wish to satisfy their curiosity about the subject. Explore the nature of the Spiritual Body, learn how to prepare yourself to be a medium, experience for yourself the trance state, clairvoyance, psychometry, table tipping and levitation, talking boards, automatic writing, spirit photography, spiritual healing, channeling, development circles, and also learn how to avoid spiritual fraud.

~~~❦~~~

"Those who read this book, and then set out to discover for themselves the positive experiences which can be found through authentic and gifted mediums today, could be rewarded with new faith for living."

— John Rossner, Ph.D.
President, International Institute of
Integral Human Services, Montréal

"Readers who seek to open 'doors to other worlds' can find no better guide than Ray Buckland's new book. Ray is careful to make clear distinctions between mediumship and channeling, then he fills the book with historical perspective, solid advice, important cautions, and numerous exercises and techniques. *Doors to Other Worlds* is at once erudite and down-to-Earth and written in Buckland's friendly one-on-one prose."

— Brad Steiger
author of *Undying Love, Starborn*

About the Author

Raymond Buckland came to the United States from England in 1962. He has been actively involved in the study of the occult for over thirty-five years. He has had twenty books published in the past twenty-three years and has lectured extensively plus appeared on numerous national and international television talk shows. He is listed in *Contemporary Authors, Who's Who In America,* and many other reference works.

To Write to the Author

If you wish to contact the author or would like more information about this book, please write to the author in care of Llewellyn Worldwide, and we will forward your request. Both the author and publisher appreciate hearing from you and learning of your enjoyment of this book and how it has helped you. Llewellyn Worldwide cannot guarantee that every letter written to the author can be answered, but all will be forwarded. Please write to:

Raymond Buckland
c/o Llewellyn Worldwide
P.O. Box 64383-06
St. Paul, MN 55164-0383, U.S.A.

Please enclosed a self-addressed, stamped envelope or $1.00 to cover costs. If outside the U.S.A., enclose international postal reply coupon.

DOORS TO
OTHER WORLDS

A Practical Guide
to Communicating with Spirits

Raymond Buckland

2000
Llewellyn Publications
St. Paul, Minnesota 55164-0383, U.S.A.

FIRST EDITION
Seventh printing, 2000

Cover Painting: Thomas Canny
Illustrations: Raymond Buckland
Photos: Raymond Buckland; Prints and Photographs Division, Library of Congress; Psychic Press, Ltd.; John and Barb Wolck
Book Design and Layout: Jessica Thoreson

Library of Congress Cataloging-in-Publication Data
    Buckland, Raymond.
        Doors to other worlds: a practical guide to communicating with spirits / Raymond Buckland.
            p.   cm.
        Includes bibliographical references.
        ISBN 0-87542-061-3
        1. Spiritualism.   I. Title.
    BF1261.2.B78   1993
    133.9—dc20   93-940
                                                      CIP

Llewellyn Worldwide does not participate in, endorse, or have any authority or responsibility concerning private business transactions between our authors and the public.
 All mail addressed to the author is forwarded but the publisher cannot, unless specifically instructed by the author, give out an address or phone number.

Llewellyn Publications
A Division of Llewellyn Worldwide, Ltd.
P.O. Box 64383, St. Paul, MN 55164-0383
www.llewellyn.com

Printed in the United States of America

**For
TARA**

**and in memory of
my father and Uncle George**

Other Books by Raymond Buckland

Llewellyn Publications

Coin Divination (April, 2000)
Gypsy Witchcraft and Magic (1998)
Gypsy Fortune Telling Tarot Kit
(book and deck, 1998)
Advanced Candle Magick (1996)
Cardinal's Sin (fiction, 1996)
Buckland Gypsies' Domino Divination Deck (1995)
Truth About Spirit Communication (1995)
The Committee (fiction, 1993)
Doors to Other Worlds (1993)
Scottish Witchcraft (1991)
Secrets of Gypsy Love Magick (1990)
Witchcraft Yesterday and Today (video, 1990)
Secrets of Gypsy Fortunetelling (1988)
Buckland's Complete Book of Witchcraft (1986)
Practical Color Magick (1983)
Witchcraft from the Inside (1971, 1975, 1995)
Practical Candleburning Rituals (1970, 1976, 1982)

Other Publishers

Ray Buckland's Magic Cauldron (Galde Press, 1995)
The Book of African Divination (Inner Traditions, 1992)
with Kathleen Binger
The Magic of Chant-O-Matics (Parker, 1978)
Anatomy of the Occult (Weiser, 1977)
Amazing Secrets of the Psychic World (Parker, 1975)
with Hereward Carrington
Here Is the Occult (HC, 1974)
The Tree: Complete Book of Saxon Witchcraft
(Weiser, 1974)
Mu Revealed (Warner Paperback Library, 1970)
under the pseudonym "Tony Earll"
Witchcraft Ancient and Modern (HC, 1970)
A Pocket Guide to the Supernatural (Ace, 1969)
Witchcraft . . . the Religion (Buckland Museum, 1966)

The distinctive contribution of Spiritualism to the enlightenment of mankind is to show that our continued existence after death is not a pious hope but a demonstrable fact.

—W. H. Mackintosh

Spiritualism will make religion infinitely more real, and translate it from the domain of belief to that of life. It has been to me, in common with many others, such a lifting of the mental horizon and a letting in of the heavens — such a transformation of faith into facts — that I can only compare life without it to sailing on board ship with hatches battened down, and being kept prisoner . . . living by the light of a candle . . . and blind to a thousand possibilities of being — and then suddenly on some starry night allowed to go on deck for the first time to see the stupendous mechanism of the starry heavens all aglow.

—Gerald Massey

Table of Contents

INTRODUCTION

Uncle George was my father's brother and someone of whom I was very fond. He was no more than five feet in height and had the most infectious laugh I have ever come across (almost a giggle, actually). He and my aunt Doris, together with my mother's brother and his wife, had left England in the early 1930s and emigrated to the United States. Unfortunately Uncle George developed health problems — the climate of New York's Long Island did not agree with him — and, just before the start of World War II, he and my aunt returned to England.

Uncle George had the most wonderful stories to tell of America, especially about Prohibition, and I would listen to him for hours. He was also an excellent artist and encouraged me in my drawing: pen and ink, pencil, and charcoal.

Uncle George and Aunt Doris were Spiritualists. I don't know if they were of that affiliation before they left for America or whether that was something they became members of during their sojourn abroad. But again and again Uncle George would regale me with wondrous stories of mediums he had witnessed and séances he had attended both in America and in England. He told of miraculous healings he had seen performed, by the late Harry Edwards and others.

When I was about twelve years old Uncle George loaned me a book on Spiritualism. I don't remember which one it was but I read it and devoured it. I asked him for more, which he was only too happy to provide. I was always a voracious reader and I quickly worked my way through all the spiritualist books he had. From there I headed for the public library.

This was the beginning of my interest in matters metaphysical. I slowly but surely worked my way along the library shelves, from spiritualism into ghosts, E.S.P., magic, witchcraft, divination, and so on. I was never to look back. Doors had been opened to me which, in turn, led to other doors; I had been introduced to a wide subject that would keep me captivated for the rest of this lifetime. I often look now at my personal library of some three thousand such books and murmur "Thank you, Uncle George!"

In my late teens and into my early twenties I found that a number of my close friends found a similar interest in the possibility of spirit contact. In my London flat we would get together once a week and work with a Ouija board, or with automatic writing or similar things. We were none of us gullible nor were we total skeptics; we kept careful notes, tried to keep open minds and carefully examined everything that happened. And some striking things did happen.

One evening we were using a board when the spirit we contacted claimed to have been a brother of mine. It (or "he") went on to say "I died new-born." I have only one brother to my knowledge and he is still alive, so I later questioned Uncle George and showed him what I had received. He told me something I had not known — and certainly no one else present could have known. He told me that my mother had had a still-born child two years before the birth of my older brother! Later my mother confirmed this.

Another time we contacted the spirit of a man who had been hanged for a murder he did not commit (or so he claimed). He gave us the name of the woman he was supposed to have killed, also the name of the church where she was buried and the year she was buried (1847, as I recall). None of us had heard of the church but a study of a map of the Greater London area confirmed that there was such a place. The following weekend we all traveled to the church and spent a good couple of hours or more moving through the cemetery studying the gravestones. We couldn't find one for the woman in question.

The church had been badly bombed during the war and many grave markers were missing. On the pretext of doing genealogical research, I wrote to the vicar and asked if he had any record of such a woman having died on such a date. I received a prompt reply. The church records had been placed in safe-keeping for the duration of the war. In checking through them, the vicar confirmed that there had indeed been a woman of the name given who was buried on that particular date in the churchyard.

To a young man such as myself, starting out along the path of psychic research, these and many other examples were enough to not only hold my interest but to start me forward on a spiritual quest. I learned that, although not Spiritualists themselves, my father and mother had traveled a similar route, holding séances with Uncle George and Aunt Doris and several other friends in the early years of their marriage, before George and Doris emigrated.

Over the many years since then I have never lost my interest in spiritualism. When I, in my turn, emigrated to the United States and took up residence on Long Island, New York, I went to occasional séances and, over several years, investigated many haunted houses there. When I bought and lived in a nineteenth century home in New Hampshire I found I was in the company of at least two ghosts, both of whom made themselves visible to me and to others. In the mid 1970s in Virginia Beach, Virginia, I held the position of Education Director for the Poseidia Institute, which was one of the early organizations working with channelers and psychics. And during my eight years in southern California I attended a number of séances at churches and at the famous Harmony Grove Spiritualist Center. It was in San Diego that I finally came to realize that I had some small gift of mediumship myself, suddenly finding myself describing long-dead friends and relatives to a group of people, some of whom I knew and some of whom were strangers to me.

In recent years I have found that more and more people are turning to spiritualism. There seems to be a veritable renaissance of interest in spiritualism, from talking boards, to séances, to all forms of mediumship. There is so much about it that "makes the most remarkable sense." Extra sensory perception, or E.S.P., has been well-proven for many years. If we are able to communicate with one another mind-to-mind, in the flesh, then why not in and out of the flesh? From earliest times teachings and writings have held that the spirit lives on after death. Then why should we not be able to make contact with that spirit? I believe that we can. By the time you have worked through this book I think you will agree with me.

Uncle George still looks down on me, as do my father and my grandfather. They have all been dead many years, yet they are all still very much a part of me. And this is one of the greatest pleasures of spiritualism — knowing that you never really lose anyone . . . not even to death.

Raymond Buckland

George Buckland

I

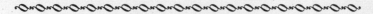

MEDIUMSHIP

Beginnings

In various of my books I have spoken of the earliest beginnings of religio-magic and described the probable actions of Paleolithic peoples in their attempts to communicate with deity. Certainly we know that the earliest humans needed success in hunting in order to survive and, from extant cave paintings, carvings and clay models, we know that "magic" was performed immediately before their all-important hunts. We also know from these sources that humankind called upon deity to bring success to this magic, thereby making these hunts fruitful.

From the painting known as "The Sorcerer" in the *Caverne des Trois Frères,* in Ariége, France, it can be seen that a member of the tribe would dress in the skins of a stag and wear the mask and horns of the animal — playing the role of the God of Hunting — in order to lead a ritual designed to bring success to the stag hunt that would follow. As part of his role the person playing the part of the Hunting God would almost certainly have spoken as that deity, directing the hunters in their pantomimed actions. And what he might well have been

1

doing — whether or not he realized it — was "channel-ing" the deity; actually allowing the Hunting God to speak through him.

Channeling

Channeling is a phenomenon that has become popular in recent years, with any number of people publicly going into trance and allowing "entities" to speak through them to their audiences. In public halls, on television, on video tapes, these channelers can be seen and heard. Though not claiming to be a plenipotentiary for "God," many of them do claim that they are bringing the voice, and the teachings, of an entity who has never previously lived on this earth but who dwells, or has dwelled, on some far distant planet or even in some other dimension.

Throughout the ages, from those early cave-dweller days continuously through to these present examples, channeling can be found. The ancient Egyptian priests would frequently play the part of one or other of their many gods and goddesses. Once again we have extant examples of the paraphernalia used, for example the mask worn when representing Anubis, the jackal-headed god. The sibyls of ancient Greece were regularly consulted by the populace who desired to speak with their deities. The Romans, too, had their soothsayers and seers, who passed on the words of the dwellers on Mount Olympus. In the Mayan temples the priests played the part of their gods, giving or relaying instruction and advice to the people.

In the Bible, in 1st Corinthians (Chapters 12 and 14) there are exhortations for all to use their gifts of prophesy and other spiritual gifts. Throughout the Middle Ages it was common to consult with those who had access to the land beyond death through the rituals of necromancy. In eighteenth and nineteenth century Haiti, the slaves developed their own form of religion — a combination of their native African beliefs and practices mixed in with those of the indigenous Indians and what they saw as the power of the Catholic Church — to produce Voodoo. In Voodoo, the sole purpose of many of the gatherings is to speak to the deities, who "appear" by possessing one or other of the worshippers and speaking through them. In modern day Panchmuda, India (northwest of Calcutta), similar rites are held each year at the Temple of Manasa for the Snake Festival, when the Serpent Mother takes possession of her worshippers.

Writers, musicians and artists have long composed through a process of channeling. Wolfgang Mozart heard music in his head and simply wrote down what he heard, never changing or correcting it. In the mid-nineteenth century came the birth of the present-day spiritualist movement, with the Fox Sisters of New York, in 1848, discovering a simple method to communicate with the spirits of the dead. (See Chapters Three and Four.)

It can be seen, then, that there is nothing new in channeling, be it bringing messages from those who have died and passed on, producing advice from extraterrestrial entities, or speaking the words of divinities.

The channel is a medium through which the information is produced. (What that information is, how accurate it may be, and from whence it comes, are questions we will address later in this book.) *Anyone* can act as a channel, or medium. Some people seem more readily attuned to the position than others, but we all have the capability. Most work consciously and have, indeed, spent time in training to achieve their results, yet some act completely spontaneously and unconsciously.

Possession

Mediumship is not the same thing as possession. In possession an undesirable spirit or entity takes over the body of a living human, forcing out and overriding that human's spirit. It possesses and refuses to give up possession unless driven out . . . though there are actually far fewer cases of true possession than late night movies and the sensational media would have you believe!

In mediumship the living human may *voluntarily* allow another spirit to make use of his or her vocal chords, hand and/or arm muscles, or whatever; never giving up total control of the entire body. It is a mutual agreement that can be terminated at any time. Under the proper circumstances there is absolutely no harm that can come to the medium, yet it may be wise to use some precautionary measures "just in case." These I will deal with, in detail, in Chapter Five.

However, in many types of mediumship there is no giving up of any of the medium's organism whatsoever. For example, with clairvoyance and clairaudience the medium is simply seeing and hearing and then relaying what he or she sees or hears. It is only in such forms as direct voice, automatic writing, and the like that there is ever any degree of use of the medium's body.

In this book I will be dealing mainly with mediumship in the sense of obtaining information from the spirits of those who have died and passed on but, towards the end of the book, I will also look into channeling of other entities.

II

THE WORLD OF SPIRIT

A 1980 Gallup Poll revealed that as many as 71% of Americans believe in an afterlife. Orthodox theology has brainwashed many of us to believe in a "Heaven" and a "Hell," as the two ultimate destinations for our soul, or spirit (I prefer the word "spirit" and will stick with that throughout this book.) The Roman Catholic Church also throws in "Purgatory" as a third intermediary state. As Hereward Carrington pointed out, in *Your Psychic Powers And How To Develop Them* (New York 1920):

> *When in this state (Purgatory), souls may be helped either by those who have passed over or by the prayers of the living. It will thus be seen that, in this respect at least, the Catholic church approaches nearer than any other religion the doctrines of Spiritualism!*

In many religions, as in Spiritualism, there is no such division into two or three parts. The afterlife is in one place, neither "good" nor "bad," having neither rewards nor punishments. Andrew Jackson Davis coined the term "Summerland" for this afterlife world. It is a place very much like our present earthly plane, yet on the next, more advanced, level of existence. The information about this next plane has come to us from a wide variety of sources and, as might be expected, is very contradictory!

Traditional Image of the Afterlife

Looking into the Spirit World

Where do these reports come from? Who gives them? In recent times a large number of "near-death experiences" have been documented. Raymond Moody and Elisabeth Kübler-Ross, among others, have written extensively on the descriptions of what has been found by people who have briefly "died" and passed over, only to return. But there have also been excursions into the spirit world, undertaken by shamans, seers and clairvoyants, for centuries. Moses, Swedenborg, Andrew Jackson Davis, and others have recorded what they have found. More importantly, perhaps, we also have a wealth of material given to us through mediums, directly from spirits of the dead, describing their new world in minute detail. From this we have a fairly complete representative picture of the spirit world.

Death will not make you omniscient. Far from it; you enter the new life still carrying with you all the beliefs, prejudices and opinions that you had here on earth. If you believed in reincarnation before death you will almost certainly find it confirmed after death. Yet, if you did *not* believe in reincarnation prior to death you are just as likely to find that "confirmed" after death!

It seems that the most devoutly religious find what they expect — an afterlife that is much as their teachings have led them to believe they will find — whereas the not-so-devout find it to be more like the physical plane they just left. How can there be this difference? It seems likely that those who have been indoctrinated with certain expectations will find those expectations satisfied, at least for a period. Then gradually, it seems, they are brought to see that not everything is exactly as they were taught. In this way there is no great shock to them on passing over. So, reincarnation — and other major beliefs — may or may not be a fact, but it will take a while

in the afterlife to find out. Just because a spirit, returning through the agencies of a medium, states that he or
she has found a particular thing to be so, does not necessarily mean that it is so.

How, then, can we judge anything that is relayed to
us through a medium? Much the same as here on earth.
We must listen to the reports, consider the majority
voice, and then go with what makes most sense to us, as
individuals. It won't be confirmed or denied until we
make that passage ourselves, and then probably not for
some time after.

It does seem certain that there are a number of levels — variously described as "zones" or "spheres" —
through which we must progress. Our rate of progres-
sion is entirely up to us. For the duration of this book I
will describe this earthly plane as the First Level and that
immediately following death as the Second Level.
Apparently communication between two adjacent levels
is easier than communication between separated levels.
In other words, it is easier for us to make contact with
those who have died relatively recently than with those
who have been dead a considerable time and have
passed on to higher levels.

Also, it is possible to "visit" a lower level (e.g., as
with a spirit from Level Two materializing briefly in Level
One), yet not possible to move up before your time to a
higher level.

Meeting "God"

All reports received through mediums seem to indicate
that spirits do not have any immediate confrontation
with any Infinite Intelligence; they do not pass directly
into the presence of God or Goddess. However, as they
progress in spiritual perception and understanding, they

do seem to gradually perceive that the universe, far from being chaotic due to pure chance, is in fact orderly and systematic. There seems the possibility of it being governed by some Supreme Intelligence. Whether or not that Intelligence, if it does exist, is eventually encountered is unknown to us here on Level One . . . and probably on the next few levels also.

The Spiritual Body

From spirit contact we learn that on the Second Level we retain the same appearance that we had here on Level One, with one exception. The exception is that we may assume the state/development of that body we most prefer. In other words, if I end life with a bald head and a paunch, I can regain the slim, trim shape of my youth merely by wishing it so! Similarly someone who went through life crippled will be fit and healthy in the afterlife.

But how is it, then, that a medium contacting your grandparents (for example) describes them as they were when they died — old and withered, with white hair and stooped shoulders? It is simply that the communicating grandparent assumes, for the time of the séance, the body by which you are most likely to remember him or her, to make recognition easier. After the séance they will almost certainly revert to their preferred appearance.

Spirit Speech and Travel

Conversation between spirits is probably on a telepathic basis. Whether or not their lips move may depend upon how long they have been on the Second Level. It's like it is in our dreams, where we can be aware of what someone is saying without their actually "mouthing" it. In our dreams this seems quite natural and so it would be in the Spirit World. When communicating through a medium, however, I'm sure that most spirits seem to speak as we do on this level, if only to facilitate the medium's reception and understanding.

The body as we know it has an invisible double, known as the *ethereal* or *astral body*. It is an exact duplicate of its physical counterpart. In fact this astral body may well be our actual "spirit." In dreams — or what we think of as dreams — the astral body travels about at will, meeting the astral bodies of others, both living and dead. Remembrance of these travels and meetings are what we later recall as "dreams."

On the astral plane, our astral bodies can move with the speed of thought. *Think* you are in a particular location and so you are . . . even if it's half way around the world. This may seem incredible until you consider the speed of such things as radio waves. These travel around the world at the speed of light — 186,000 miles a second; the equivalent of traveling four hundred fifty times around the world in one minute! Such being the case, it is not unreasonable to accept that thought can move just as fast.

And, as with thought, so with the spirits of the dead. They can relocate as fast as thinking.

Other Life Forms

In shamanism it is accepted that all things have spirits — *all things,* be they animal, vegetable or mineral. Certainly if you break all things down to their atomic and then sub-atomic levels, they are mostly space with little obvious difference between animal, vegetable or mineral. This space could well be the "spirit" in shamanism which is found in all things, and by which all things are interconnected in the web of life.

What we perceive as a tree in this world is only the outward manifestation of the real spiritual tree lying within it, and this is true of all physical manifestations which we see in nature. Every physical body has a corresponding spiritual body behind it. Indeed, this fact gave rise to the famous "Doctrine of Correspondences" put forth by Swedenborg. As Hereward Carrington says:

> *This correspondence throws a little light on the bewildering fact that spirits often speak of spirit-gold, spirit-marble, spirit-houses, spirit-books, etc., as if they were tangible realities — not, of course, that these are sublimations of corresponding objects of earth, existent throughout but different as to material, yet sufficiently alike to be called by the same name. In other words, these spirit-objects are expressed in a different vehicle of the nature which is to us, externalized as gold, marble, etc. . . . We must endeavor to realize the reality of the spiritual world, which we have been unaccustomed to think of as in any way substantial owing to the teachings of theology.*

"Evil" Entities

I will speak more on the possibility of encountering anything "evil" in the Spirit World in Chapter Five. But for now let us consider that negative forces traditionally seem drawn to the darkness and positive forces to the light. As we progress, we speak of "the light dawning," and of "coming into the light." This does not necessarily mean that we emerge from a material darkness and enter a material light, but rather that we go through a process of psychic evolution corresponding to this. Yet in near-death experiences, those who have "died" and returned always seem to speak of entering a tunnel of bright light, often so bright that they cannot see what is at the end of it. Very literally, "coming into the light."

Spiritually and parapsychologically, we speak of moving "lost souls," "earthbound spirits," "ghosts," forward into the light, so that they may progress.

Transition

What happens at the moment of death? Many people are afraid of dying, yet it seems there is really no need for this fear. One of the joys of spiritualism, to my mind, is that it proves the continuance of existence after death and thereby removes the primary fear of ending everything. As will be seen in progressing through this book, even communication with loved ones is not necessarily ended at death.

In astral projection, our ethereal double slips out of our physical body and goes on its way, preserving its connection to the physical with an infinitely elastic silver-colored cord. When we dream there, too, our invisible double slides out of its shell and goes off, stretching its cord behind it. Well, at death it is the same process; the spirit separates from the physical shell and leaves. The only difference is that at death there is no preserved connection by the cord. It has separated, and therefore there is no going back.

It would be interesting to know if, in cases of the "near-death experience" — where someone has to all intents and purposes "died" yet later comes back — the silver cord is there or not. My suspicion would be that yes, it is still there.

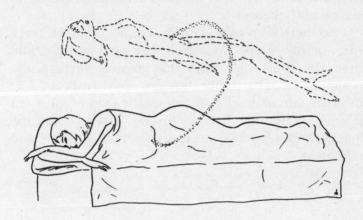

Physical and Astral Bodies

Here is a typical death experience related by a departed spirit speaking through a medium:

> *When I awoke in the spirit-life and saw that I still had hands and feet and all the rest of the human body, I can't say what feelings took hold of me. I realized that I had this body . . . a spiritual body, but a body. Imagine being re-born, free from the decaying flesh. I gazed on weeping friends with a saddened heart, mingled with joy, knowing that I could still be with them daily, though unseen and unheard. Then I felt a light touch on my shoulder and turned to find many loved ones who had long since departed life on earth; all there to greet me and help me move on.*

Many records of near-death experiences speak of leaving the body, going towards a bright light — oftimes down a sort of tunnel — and seeing deceased loved ones there. In these experiences these loved ones often told the spirit to return, that the time had not yet come to pass completely over.

So there is no pain in death. On the contrary, there is frequently escape from pain. The moment of death, when the spirit slips from the physical shell, is the moment that any pain that was present disappears. The only real pain of death is, in reality, the pain of those left behind, believing that they have forever lost the deceased. But for that deceased there is now joy and happiness.

III

<O><O><O><O><O><O><O><O><O><O><O><O><O><O><O><O>

THE HISTORY OF SPIRITUALISM: THE EARLY YEARS

The Episode at Hydesville

As I stated in Chapter One, spiritualist phenomena have been manifesting for thousands of years. The ancient Greek oracles channeled by going into trance and speaking with a changed voice and personality. The sixteenth century Tremblers of Cevennes, Germany, went into trance, spoke in tongues, communicated with spirits and cured sickness. In the Bible the "Woman of Endor" (it was only King James who labeled her a "Witch;" nowhere in the text is she so described) is an out-and-out spiritualist medium, producing exactly the same phenomena that mediums have been regularly producing in the séance rooms for the past one hundred fifty years.

But the modern spiritualist movement was more firmly established — founded, if you like — in 1848, in the state of New York, as the result of publicity afforded the happenings at the Fox homestead, in Hydesville, Wayne County.

Ever since moving into the house on December 11, 1847, the Fox family had been plagued with strange sounds echoing through the wooden cottage. There

15

were knockings and rappings, the origins of which neither John Fox nor his wife Margaret were able to trace.
They tried all the obvious possibilities, such as loose
shutters and window sashes, frequently getting up in the
middle of the night to go searching through the house,
candle in hand.

On the night of Friday, March 31, they and their
two daughters had just retired to bed when the noises
once again started up — in particular, what sounded like
someone or something rapping sharply on wood. Here is
a statement made by Mrs. Margaret Fox:

> It was very early when we went to bed on this night
> — hardly dark. I had been so broken of rest I was
> almost sick . . . I had just lain down. It commenced
> as usual. I knew it from all the other noises I had
> ever heard before. The children, who slept in the
> other bed in the room, heard the rapping, and tried
> to make similar sounds by snapping their fingers.
>
> My youngest child, Cathie, said: "Mr. Splitfoot, do
> as I do," clapping her hands. The sound instantly
> followed her with the same number of raps. When she
> stopped the sound ceased for a short time. Then
> Margaretta said, in sport: "No, do just as I do.
> Count one, two, three, four," striking one hand
> against the other at the same time; and the raps
> came as before. She was afraid to repeat them . . .
>
> I then thought I could put a test that no one in the
> place could answer. I asked the "noise" to rap my
> different children's ages successively. Instantly, each
> one of my children's ages was given correctly, paus-
> ing between them sufficiently long to individualise
> them until the seventh, at which a longer pause was
> made, and then three more emphatic raps were

given, corresponding to the age of the little one that died, which was my youngest child.

I then asked: "Is this a human being that answers my questions so correctly?" There was no rap. I asked: "Is it a spirit? If it is, make two raps." Two sounds were given as soon as the request was made.

The Foxes went on with their questions and slowly learned that the spirit was a thirty-one year old man, a peddler, who had been murdered in the house. Mrs. Fox asked "Will you continue to rap if I call in my neighbors, that they may hear it too?" The raps were affirmative. She called in her neighbor, Mrs. Redfield. The testimony continues:

Mrs. Redfield is a very candid woman. The girls were sitting up in bed clinging to each other and trembling with terror . . . Mrs. Redfield came immediately (this was about half past seven), thinking she would have a laugh at the children. But when she saw them pale with fright and nearly speechless, she was amazed and believed there was something more serious than she had supposed. I asked a few questions for her and she was answered as before. He told her age exactly. She then called her husband, and the same questions were asked and answered.

The Foxes went on to call in the Dueslers, the Hydes, the Jewells and several others.

On first looking at the phenomenon it would seem to be typical of poltergeist activity. There were young children in the house; Margaretta was seven and Cathie, or Kate, ten years of age. With children of that age it is not uncommon for there to be spontaneous physical activity brought about by raw energy, for want of a better word, thrown off by the children. But the Fox episode differs from "normal" poltergeist activity in that the noises responded intelligently to questions. Indeed, they acknowledged being a "spirit." Poltergeist activity is completely unpredictable and uncontrollable, so here was a very real difference.

It is a little-known fact that the house had a prior history of strange noises. The tenants previous to the Foxes were a Michael and Hannah Weekman, who vacated the premises because of the noises. Before the Weekmans was a couple named Bell.

With the crowd of neighbors in the house that Friday night, the spirit was thoroughly tested with questions of all sorts. All were answered to the satisfaction of the questioners. The spirit also gave all the details of his murder, which was done with a butcher knife and in order to steal his money. Margaret Fox and the two girls left for the night, leaving the house overflowing with people, and still the rappings continued.

The next evening, Saturday, it was said that as many as three hundred people gathered to witness the rappings. The spirit claimed that its body had been buried ten feet below the surface of the ground. Immediate excavations turned up hair and bones, pronounced by medical experts to be human. But it wasn't until fifty-six years later that the whole skeleton was discovered. According to a report in the *Boston Journal* of November 23, 1904, parts of a basement wall collapsed and revealed an entire human skeleton . . . together with a peddler's tin box!

Earlier a maid, named Lucretia Pulver, who had worked for the Bells when they lived in the house, testified that she remembered a peddler once stopping there. Lucretia was sent off for the night and when she

The Famous Fox Sisters
(Photo courtesy Prints and Photographs Division,
Library of Congress)

returned the next morning she was told the peddler had left. The Bells were never charged with the murder. In her statement Lucretia said that both she and a friend, Aurelia Losey, had subsequently heard strange noises during the night in the house.

Andrew Jackson Davis

The birth of spiritualism, in the Fox home, had been predicted. On that same March 31, 1848, a man who became known as the "Poughkeepsie Seer" wrote in his journal:

> About daylight this morning a warm breathing passed over my face and I heard a voice, tender and strong, saying: "Brother, the good work has begun — behold a living demonstration is born." I was left wondering what could be meant by such a message.

Obviously it referred to the Hydesville rappings.

Andrew Jackson Davis was born in 1826 and grew up with little schooling. In his first sixteen years he only read one book, yet by the time he was twenty he was to write what Sir Arthur Conan Doyle has called "one of the most profound and original books of philosophy ever produced."

At the age of twelve Davis started to hear voices, giving him advice. On this advice he convinced his father to leave their native Blooming Grove, on the Hudson, and move to Poughkeepsie. His father was a weaver then later became a shoemaker. A year or so later Davis began seeing things: at his mother's death he saw a beautiful house in a wonderful land of brightness, and knew it was where his mother had gone.

Andrew Jackson Davis
(Photo courtesy Prints and Photographs Division,
Library of Congress)

A travelling showman introduced Davis to hypnotism. It was found that while in trance the boy had tremendous clairvoyant powers. So much so that a local tailor named Levingston quit his profession to work fulltime with Davis, diagnosing disease. Davis said that the human body became transparent to his spirit eyes — which actually seemed to work from the position of the third eye. Each organ then stood out clearly and with a radiance that was only dimmed by disease. He was also able to diagnose at a distance; his astral body soaring away over the land to the person whose body he needed to review.

One day in 1844, Davis suddenly left his native Poughkeepsie and, in a state of semi-trance, wandered forty miles away into the Catskill Mountains. He later claimed that while there he met and talked with the spirits of Claudius Galen, a second century Greek physician, and Emanuel Swedenborg. Swedenborg was a brilliant eighteenth century Swedish seer who was the first to explain that death means no change; that the spirit world is a counterpart of this world.

In 1845, in his nineteenth year, Davis felt the need to write a book. He broke his partnership with Levingston and teamed up with a Dr. Lyon, from Bridgeport, as hypnotist for this work. Lyon gave up his practice and took the young man to New York, where a Reverend William Fishbough also gave up his work to act as secretary and take the dictation Davis gave while in trance. In November 1845 Davis began to dictate his great work: *The Principles of Nature, Her Divine Revelations, and a Voice to Mankind.* The dictation lasted for fifteen months.

A professor of Hebrew at the University of New York, Dr. George Bush, was present at many of the trance utterings. He later said:

I can solemnly affirm that I have heard Davis correctly quote the Hebrew language in his lectures (dictation), and display a knowledge of geology which would have been astonishing in a person of his age, even if he had devoted years to the study. He has discussed, with the most signal ability, the profoundest questions of historical and Biblical archaeology, of mythology, of the origin and affinity of language, and the progress of civilization among the different nations of the globe, which would do honor to any scholar of the age, even if in reaching them he had the advantage of access to all the libraries of Christendom. Indeed, if he had acquired all the information he gives forth in these lectures, not in the two years since he left the shoemaker's bench, but in his whole life, with the most assiduous study, no prodigy of intellect of which the world has ever heard would be for a moment compared with him, yet not a single volume or page has he ever read.

By the time he was twenty-one Davis no longer needed a hypnotist, being able to put himself into light trance. Later still his writing was purely inspirational. He attracted the attention of numerous famous personalities, Edgar Allan Poe among them, and became a prolific author. His psychic development went on. One time he sat beside a dying woman and observed every detail of her spirit's departure from the body, detailing it in his book *The Great Harmonia* (1852).

Much of Davis' work reflected Swedenborg's earlier thoughts but, as Sir Arthur Conan Doyle said:

They went one step farther, having added just that knowledge of spirit power which Swedenborg may have attained after his death . . . Is it not a feasible hypothesis that the power which controlled Davis was actually Swedenborg? . . . But whether Davis stood alone, or whether he was the reflection of one greater than himself, the fact remains that he was a miracle man . . . (who) left his mark deep upon Spiritualism.

—The History Of Spiritualism (1924)

The Fox Sisters

The Fox family had been greatly disturbed by the events at the house. Margaret Fox's hair turned white within a week of the affair. The two children were sent away; Kate to stay with her brother David, in Auburn, and Margaretta to stay with her sister Leah (married name Fish), in Rochester. But "the raps continued in the house even after they had left" (*Encyclopedia of Psychic Science*, Nandor Fodor, London 1934).

A stranger factor was now to appear . . . not only did the raps continue at the house, but they also followed the girls to their new abodes. In Rochester, Leah, a staid music teacher, was suddenly exposed to violent disturbances. The phenomenon reverted back to poltergeist-like outbursts, with Margaretta and Leah the targets of flying blocks of wood and pinpricks. Leah said that:

Pins would be stuck into various parts of our persons. Mother's cap would be removed from her head, her comb jerked out of her hair and every conceivable thing done to annoy us.

It took a while for them to remember that they had been able to converse with the spirit in the Hydesville house, through asking for raps in answer to questions.

They started to ask questions again, and once again they got answers. Then they got the most important message of all:

> *Dear friends, you must proclaim this truth to the world. This is the dawning of a new era. You must not try to conceal it any longer. When you do your duty, God will protect you and good spirits will watch over you.*

From that moment messages started to pour forth.

On November 14, 1849, a group of people met at the Corinthian Hall in Rochester and a panel was formed to investigate the girls. This panel determined that there was no fraud involved in what was produced. However, many present were not satisfied with this report and demanded that a second committee be formed. This was done and the second group reached a similar conclusion. They stated that when the girls were "standing on pillows, with a handkerchief tied round the bottom of their dresses tight to the ankles, we all heard rapping on the wall and floor distinctly."

As interest in the phenomenon spread so it was found that other people were able to act as channels, or "mediums," for the spirits. Leah's ability developed and she found herself so much in demand that she had to give up her music teaching and became the first professional medium.

The sisters started a tour, going to Albany in May of 1850 and then on to Troy. In June they were in New York. There Horace Greeley, editor of the *New York Tribune,* investigated them. He was joined by Fenimore Cooper, George Bancroft, the poets Willis and Bryant, and others. Greeley reported in his newspaper:

We devoted what time we could spare from our duties
out of three days to this subject, and it would be the
basest cowardice not to say that we are convinced
beyond a doubt of their perfect integrity and good
faith in the premises. Whatever may be the origin or
cause of the "rappings," the ladies in whose presence
they occur do not make them. We tested this thor-
oughly and to our entire satisfaction.

The early rappings gave way to other phenomena;
table tipping, automatic writing, materialization and
even levitation. In 1853 it was reported that Governor
Talmadge was levitated while sitting on a table! The governor also claimed that he had received direct writing
from the spirit of John C. Calhoun.

Mediums started springing up all over the place.
Not surprisingly many of them were exposed as frauds.
The phenomena were of the sort that *could* be produced
fraudulently and therefore many charlatans tried to
jump on "the bandwagon." Exposures became almost
commonplace and finally even reached out towards the
Fox sisters themselves. They were accused of producing
the raps by "cracking" their knee joints and toe joints! In
fact an alleged "confession" was presented by a relative, a
Mrs. Norman Culver, who claimed that Catherine had
told her this was how they worked. In trying to explain
how the raps could continue at an investigation where
the committee held the ankles of the sisters, Mrs. Culver
said that they had their servant rap on the floorboards
from down in the cellar.

There were several problems with this accusation.
The investigations in question had been held at the
homes of various members of the committee plus in a
public hall, and at that time the Fox sisters didn't even
have a servant! Not only that, but a Mr. Capron was able

to show that at the time of the so-called "confession," Kate Fox was actually residing at his home, seventy miles distant!

Unfortunately the accusations did damage the reputation of the Fox sisters and for a time they found themselves with few defenders, other than Horace Greeley.

There was tremendous pressure put upon the sisters at this time; pressure to "perform." Precautions for mediumship were then unknown. In her *Autobiography,* Mrs. Hardinge Britten speaks of talking to Kate Fox at a spiritualist gathering and describes her as:

> *Poor patient Kate, in the midst of a captious, grumbling crowd of investigators, repeating hour after hour the letters of the alphabet, while the no less poor, patient spirits rapped out names, ages and dates to suit all comers.*

Interestingly, although the method of producing the sounds was frequently questioned, and many and marvelous explanations were forthcoming, seldom did anyone question the incredible amount of information that was produced; information that was unobtainable elsewhere and which, invariably, was absolutely correct. For example, from 1861 to 1866 Kate worked exclusively for the New York banker Charles F. Livermore, bringing him endless messages and information from his late wife, Estelle. During all that time Estelle actually materialized and also wrote notes in her own handwriting; all information that would have been unknown to Kate but which Livermore was able to accept.

In 1852 Margaretta married the famous Arctic explorer, Dr. Elisha Kane. In November 1858, Leah married her third husband, David Underhill, a wealthy insurance man.

In 1871 Kate visited England, where the first Spiritualist church had been established in Keighley, Yorkshire, in 1853. Her trip was financed by Livermore, in gratitude for the years of consolation that she had brought him. He wrote:

> Miss Fox, taken all in all, is no doubt the most wonderful living medium. Her character is irreproachable and pure. I have received so much through her powers of mediumship during the past ten years which is solacing, instructive and astounding, that I feel greatly indebted to her . . .

In England Kate sat for the well known psychic investigator and physicist Professor William Crookes, among others (Sir William Crookes invented the tube that made possible the development of x-rays). At one of the séances a *London Times* correspondent was present. In light of the earlier accusations made against the Fox sisters, claiming that they made the rapping noises with their joints, it is interesting to read the *Times'* correspondent's report. He says that he was taken to the door of the séance room and invited to stand by the medium and hold her hands. This he did, "when loud thumps seemed to come from the panels, as if done with the fist. These were repeated at our request any number of times." He went on to give every test he could think of, while Kate gave every opportunity for examination and had both her feet and hands held securely.

Of one séance Crookes wrote:

> I was holding the medium's two hands in one of mine, while her feet rested on my feet. Paper was on the table before us, and my disengaged hand was holding a pencil. A luminous hand came down from the upper part of the room, and after hovering near

Sir William Crookes
(Photo courtesy Prints and Photographs Division,
Library of Congress)

me for a few seconds, took the pencil from my hand,
rapidly wrote on a sheet of paper, threw the pencil
down, and then rose over our heads, gradually fad-
ing into darkness.

In December 1872 Kate married H. D. Jancken, a
London barrister and one of England's early Spiritualists. They were to have two sons, both of whom were
extremely psychic, before Jancken died in 1881. In 1876
Margaretta came across the Atlantic to visit her sister.

Denunciation and Retraction

A quarrel developed between the three sisters, with Kate
and Margaretta eventually siding together against the
older Leah. Hearing of a growing problem of alcoholism
in her sisters — especially Margaretta — Leah tried to
have Kate separated from her two children. It has been
suggested by such people as Sir Arthur Conan Doyle that
this may have prompted an attack by Margaretta, who
had been through some severe financial problems.
(Additionally she had come under strong Roman
Catholic influence, pressuring her to acknowledge that
her gift was in fact a gift from the devil!) Margaretta
swore to avenge herself and her sister against Leah.

Thinking to hurt Leah by harming the entire spiritualist movement, Margaretta wrote a letter to the *New
York Herald* in which she denounced the movement and
promised a full exposure of it. This she tried to do
before a panel, in August 1888. The following month
Kate came over from England to join her. Although she
did not promise any exposé, Kate did seem to back her
sister in the fight against Leah. In the Hall of Music, on
October 21, 1888, Margaretta made her repudiation,

claiming that all had been fake. She even managed to produce some minor raps to back up what she was saying. Kate kept silent, though by doing so seemed to endorse her sister's statements.

Suddenly, on November 17, less than a month later, Kate wrote to a Mrs. Cottell:

> *I would have written to you before this but my surprise was so great on my arrival to hear of Maggie's exposure of Spiritualism that I had no heart to write to anyone.*

> *The manager of the affair engaged the Academy of Music, the very largest place of entertainment in New York City; it was filled to overflowing. They made fifteen hundred dollars clear.*

> *I think now I could make money in proving that the knockings are not made with the toes. So many people come to me to ask me about this exposure of Maggie's that I have to deny myself to them. They are hard at work to expose the whole thing if they can; but they certainly cannot.*

On November 20, 1889, about a year after the "exposé," Margaretta gave an interview to the New York press:

> *Would to God that I could undo the injustice I did the cause of Spiritualism when, under the strong psychological influence of persons inimical to it, I gave expression to utterances that had no foundation in fact. This retraction and denial has not come about so much from my own sense of what is right as from the silent impulse of the spirits using my organism at the expense of the hostility of the treacherous horde who held out promises of wealth*

and happiness in return for an attack on Spiritual-
ism, and whose hopeful assurances were so deceitful.

She was asked "Was there any truth in the charges
you made against Spiritualism?" To which she replied:

Those charges were false in every particular. I have
no hesitation in saying that . . . When I made those
dreadful statements I was not responsible for my
words. Its genuineness is an incontrovertible fact.

Asked what her sister Catherine thought of her present course, she said: "She is in complete sympathy with
me. She did not approve my course in the past."

The three Fox sisters died within a year or two of
each other; Leah in 1890, Catherine in 1892 and Margaretta in 1893. The final word on them comes from a
woman doctor — not a spiritualist — who attended on
Margaretta at her death. At a meeting of the Medico
Legal Society of New York, in 1905, Dr. Mellen stated
that Margaretta was lying in a bed in a tenement house
on Ninth Street. According to the doctor she was
unable, at that time, to move hand or foot. Yet knockings came from the wall, the floor and from the ceiling,
in answer to Margaretta's faint questions. "She was as
incapable of cracking her toe-joints at this time, as I
was," said the doctor.

IV

THE HISTORY OF SPIRITUALISM:
LATER DEVELOPMENT

At first glance it would seem surprising that so many
fully developed mediums came forward so shortly after
the "birth" of spiritualism through the Fox sisters. But
Sir Arthur Conan Doyle explains it this way:

> *It was no new gift (the Fox sisters) exhibited, it was
> only that their courageous action in making it
> widely known made others come forward and con-
> fess that they possessed the same power. This univer-
> sal gift of mediumistic faculties now for the first
> time began to be freely developed.*

As Judge John W. Edmonds had said earlier (*Spiritualism*, New York 1853):

> *For the previous ten or twelve years there had been
> more or less of (mediumship) in different parts of
> the country, but it had been kept concealed, either
> from fear of ridicule or from ignorance of what it
> was.*

Ridicule was a major factor. As mentioned in the
previous chapter, many of the phenomena of spiritualism were easily duplicated by the unscrupulous. There
were scandals and exposures galore, both real and fab-
ricated. One major scandal was that involving Professor

Robert Hare, one of the best known scientists of the time. He had to give up his professorship at Pennsylvania University and was publicly denounced by the professors of Harvard. But the scientists made fools of themselves. As Conan Doyle describes it:

> The crowning and most absurd instance of scientific intolerance — an intolerance which has always been as violent and unreasonable as that of the mediaeval Church — was shown by the American Scientific Association. This learned body howled down Professor Hare when he attempted to address them, and put it on record that the subject was unworthy of their attention . . . however . . . the same society at the same session held an animated debate as to why cocks crow between twelve and one at night, coming finally to the conclusion that at that particular hour a wave of electricity passes over the earth from north to south, and that the fowls, disturbed out of their slumbers, and "being naturally of a crowing disposition" registered the event in this fashion!

One important development was that of private mediumship, in the sense of those who found they had mediumistic ability but did not exhibit it in public, using it for their own private purposes. A large number of men and women, many of them well known in other circles, discovered an ability to communicate with the spirits and proceeded to do so in their own homes, with only family and close friends in attendance.

Development in England

In 1852 an American medium named Mrs. Hayden visited England, followed shortly after by a Mrs. Roberts. Although they both did very well financially, they received mixed reviews. Some prominent men and women attested to the genuineness of their phenomena while others found it very difficult to accept.

By the following year the continental craze of table tipping reached English shores and became very popular. So popular, in fact, that scientists such as Faraday, Braid and Carpenter took notice and talked of it in terms of odylic force, electricity and magnetism.

There then followed a slight slump in interest until 1855, when Scottish-born Daniel Dunglas Home (pronounced *Hume)* arrived there from America. He had been practicing for several years and was to develop into one of the finest mediums of all time. He stayed only a short while but returned four years later, to stay. Home was responsible for the acceptance of spiritualism by such figures as Thackeray, Anthony Trollope, Robert Bell, Lord Lytton, Lord Adare, The Earl of Dunraven, The Master of Lindsay and Lord Brougham.

Perhaps the most famous of Home's feats was his levitation out of one window and in at another, seventy feet above the ground. It occurred at Ashley House, Victoria Street, London. Present were Lord Adare the sporting young Irish peer, his cousin Captain Charles Wynne and the Honorable Master of Lindsay (later Earl of Crawford and Balcarres). Both Adare and Lindsay wrote separate accounts of what happened that evening.

After a normal beginning to the séance — normal for Home's séances, that is, with telekinetic phenomena and the appearance of an apparition — Home began to pace the floor. He was in a trance state, as he had been

Daniel Dunglas Home (1833-86)
(Photo courtesy Prints and Photographs Division,
Library of Congress)

all evening. He walked through to the next room and a window was heard to be raised. Lindsay states that he heard a voice whisper in his ear, telling him that Home would pass out of one window and in at another. The next moment they all saw Home floating in the air outside their window.

There was no ledge of any sort between the windows, which were nearly eight feet apart and seventy feet above the ground. Although there was no light on in the room, the moon provided sufficient illumination for all to distinguish each other and to see quite clearly the furniture in the room.

After remaining in position for a few seconds outside the window, with his feet about six inches above the sill, Home opened the window and "glided into the room feet foremost." Adare went to close the window in the adjacent room and found that it had only been opened twelve to fifteen inches. Home was asked how he had managed to pass through so small a space, and replied by showing them. Adare describes it: ". . . he then went through the open space, head first, quite rapidly, his body being nearly horizontal and apparently rigid. He came in again, feet foremost; and we returned to the other room." Later, when Home came out of his trance, he was "much agitated; he said he felt as if he had gone through some fearful peril, and that he had a most horrible desire to throw himself out of the window."

Other mediums arrived from America, amongst them Mrs. Emma Hardinge Britten, the Davenport brothers, Lottie Fowler and Henry Slade. By that time the focus was on spirits actually speaking through the medium, rather than conversing by way of raps. Slate-writing was also introduced, as was billet reading, spirit photography, apports and telekinetic demonstrations.

In December of 1861 Queen Victoria's beloved husband, Prince Albert, died. Within days a young boy named Robert James Lees, living in Leicester, went into trance and received a message from the departed Prince. The message was for the Queen and was published by a newspaper editor who happened to be at the séance with Lees. Queen Victoria already had an interest in spiritualist matters and, seeing the report, sent two representatives to see Lees. The two used false names. The boy again channeled information from Prince Albert, recognized the two royal visitors and called them by their correct names. He went on to write a letter to the Queen, while in trance, in which he called Her Majesty by a private name used only by the husband and wife. The Queen was so impressed she had the thirteen-year-old Lees brought to court and held several séances with him. Later her personal manservant, John Brown, took over as the medium through whom Albert chose to speak with her. Lees went on to become one of Britain's leading mediums.

It took a while for the native English mediums to stand up and be recognized. Among the first were Mrs. Marshall, Mrs. Everitt, Edward Childs, William Howitt, William Wilkinson and Mrs. Guppy. The British National Association of Spiritualists was founded in 1873 (reorganized in 1884 as the London Spiritualist Alliance), the Psychological Society of Great Britain in 1875, and the prestigious Society for Psychical Research in 1882.

Professor Henry Sidgwick was the first President of the S.P.R. He was, at that time, the most influential professor at Cambridge University. In his first presidential address, Professor Sidgwick said:

> *We are all agreed that the present state of things is a scandal to the enlightened age in which we live, that*

*the dispute as to the reality of these marvellous phe-
nomena of which it is quite impossible to exaggerate
the scientific importance, if only a tenth part of what
has been alleged by generally credible witnesses could
be shown to be true — I say it is a scandal that the
dispute as to the reality of these phenomena should
still be going on, that so many competent witnesses
should have declared their belief in them, that so
many others should be so profoundly interested in
having the question determined, and yet the edu-
cated world, as a body, should still be simply in an
attitude of incredulity.*

The S.P.R. did important work with many well
known researchers over the years, continuously investigating. However, it did later suffer severe criticism for its
slowness, especially in investigating physical phenomena.

Many other organizations sprang up over the years,
including the Marylebone Association of Spiritualists,
the British College of Psychic Science, London Spiritualist Alliance, The British Spiritualist Lyceum Union, The
Spiritualist National Union and the Spiritualist Association of Great Britain.

Up until 1951 it was possible for any séance to be
raided by the police and for the medium to be arrested
and charged with fraud . . . under the old Witchcraft Act
of 1735! In 1951 the Witchcraft Act was finally repealed
and replaced by the Fraudulent Mediums Act (see
Appendix). This stated that mediumship was legal so
long as it was not done "with intent to deceive," or used
"any fraudulent device." Modern day fake mediums have
been charged under this new Act, a good example being
the case of Helen Duncan, repeatedly caught in fraud,
usually in materializations.

Development in America

There was a brief period where spirit communication was claimed as the basis for various free-love and community property groups, such as John Murray Spear's New Motor movement and Reverend Scott and Thomas Lake Harris' Mountain Cove Settlement. Certainly the simple rappings of the Fox sisters paled beside the sudden panorama of psychic phenomena: phantom hands, levitation, psychometry, full form materializations, slate writing, pellet reading, spirit photography and the playing of musical instruments by ghostly hands.

In 1873 there was the first camp meeting, at Lake Pleasant, Massachusetts; in 1885 there was the foundation of the American Society for Psychical Research (today having nearly three thousand members and a library of over nine thousand volumes).

Two of the most striking mediums to come forward were Mrs. Leonore E. Piper and Mina Stinson Crandon — known as "Margery."

Mrs. Piper (1859-1950), described as "the foremost trance medium in the history of psychical research," (*Encyclopedia of Occultism and Parapsychology*, Leslie A. Shepard, editor, Avon, New York 1978) was the cause of the conversion to spiritualism of such eminent people as Sir Oliver Lodge, Dr. Richard Hodgson and Professor James Hyslop. Her mediumship started at the age of eight, when she received word from the spirit world of the death of an aunt. At age twenty-two she married William Piper, of Boston. Professor James investigated her mediumship, as did Dr. Richard Hodgson. Hodgson has been described as "the keenest fraud-hunter, the most pronounced skeptic, (who) took every precaution to bar the possibility of deception." In 1898 Professor James wrote (*Psychological Review*):

Dr. Hodgson considers that the hypothesis of fraud
cannot be seriously maintained. I agree with him
absolutely. The medium has been under observation,
much of the time under close observation, as to most
of the conditions of her life, by a large number of per-
sons, eager, many of them, to pounce upon any sus-
picious circumstance for (nearly) fifteen years.

Indeed, for decades Mrs. Piper was subjected to the most stringent of tests and was never once found wanting.

"Margery" was also from Boston and was the wife of Dr. L. R. G. Crandon, Professor of Surgery at the Harvard Medical School for sixteen years. Margery's first sitting took place in May, 1923. She showed great ability at table tipping but quickly developed to trance and direct voice. Automatic writing, psychic music and other spectacular phenomena followed. A group from Harvard, including Prof. William McDougall, Dr. Gardner Murphy and Dr. Roback, started investigating Margery. She was subsequently given rigorous examination by groups in France and England. With the strictest of controls she continued to produce outstanding phenomena (in London, investigator Harry Price had developed a fraud-proof table; in ordinary light Margery twice levitated it to a height of six inches or more).

A *Scientific American* committee used instruments such as sealed glass jars, scales and electric bells to test Margery. Dr. E. J. Dingwall, as part of another committee, stated:

Phenomena occurred hitherto unrecorded in mediu-
mistic history . . . the mediumship remains one of the
most remarkable in the history of psychical research.

It is recorded that Abraham Lincoln was very much into spiritualism, attending séances in New York with J. B. Conklin and in Washington, D.C. with Mrs. Cranston

Laurie and Nettie Colburn (later to become Mrs. May-nard). Nettie, who was in her late teens at the time, went into trance at one Washington séance attended by Lincoln, and approached the President. She told him, in eloquent words, of the importance of emancipating the slaves. When she came out of trance she was so overcome at finding herself standing talking to the President that she ran off. However, on a subsequent visit to the Laurie residence, Lincoln was again lectured by the entranced Nettie and again she emphasized the necessity to free the slaves. She also stated that from the time of such a proclamation from him there would be no defeat of the Union army. As it turned out, after Lincoln did issue his proclamation on September 22, 1862, there was nothing but Union army success.

The present day legal position of mediums varies from state to state, there being no equivalent to the British Fraudulent Mediums Act in the United States. For this reason, if no other, most mediums go under the somewhat protective shell of ordination; adopting the religious title of "Reverend."

Development Circles

On both sides of the Atlantic ordinary people were drawn to this new phenomenon of communion with the spirits of the dead. Groups of people, many times just family members, got together to "sit in circle" and try to develop their own mediumistic talents. Frequently the circles were started by people who had heard the claims of the spiritualists, or had attended a demonstration, and whose curiosity led to trying to make contact themselves. With no television to distract them(!) these circles would often continue for years, and a number of fine mediums came into being as a result of them. In England there is still a great interest in these home circles; more so than in America, it seems.

A big boost — if that is the right word — was given to the spiritualist movement with the start of the Second World War. This was a time when young men were being killed on the battlefields; when wives and mothers were losing those they loved. Spiritualism offered a means to renew contact, if only temporarily, and to find satisfaction in the knowledge that there was indeed a life after death. The time between the two wars was one of the most active for spiritualism.

Spiritualism as a Religion

Before the end of the nineteenth century many spiritualist organizations were calling themselves "churches," though the Roman Catholic Church early on decided that spiritualist phenomena were the work of the devil (notwithstanding 1st Corinthians Chapters 12 and 14). The Anglicans were more tolerant, though far from actively promoting mediumship. Indeed, in 1953 there was the establishment of the Churches' Fellowship for Psychical and Spiritual Studies. The Fellowship organized conferences and study groups, lectures and workshops, dealing with mediumship, healing and psychic development.

On the whole, however, the organized churches were against spiritualism. Yet to the spiritualists themselves there was an undeniable link between proof of survival and many of the church teachings. And certainly a number of the returning spirits took the opportunity to preach the beliefs they had held while in their physical shells!

Not all spiritualist organizations wanted religious affiliation. The Spiritualists' National Union has consistently refused to adopt specific Christian doctrine. So much so, in fact, that it led to the formation, in 1931, of the Greater World Christian Spiritualist League. The S.N.U. is the largest national organization in Britain and, although organized in "churches," represents the non-Christian element in spiritualism. The G.W.C.S.L. represents the Christian element. In America groups include the National Spiritual Alliance of the United States of America, the National Spiritualist Association of Churches, the National Spiritualist Association of the United States and the Universal Spiritualist Association. Internationally there are the International Spiritualist Federation (headquartered in Paris, France) and the International General Assembly of Spiritualists.*

In America today there is more of a tie-in with religion — specifically Christianity — than is found in Britain, with many Spiritualist churches having regular services of hymns, prayers, Bible-reading and sermons along with their message-giving. Yet spiritualism remains a movement rather than an organization, with a large number of totally independent groups and autonomous "churches."

Conan Doyle said:

> *Spiritualism is a religion for those who find themselves outside all religions; while on the contrary it greatly strengthens the faith of those who already possess religious beliefs.*

* Throughout this book I use "spiritualism" with the lower-case "s" when referring to the general practice, and with a capital "S" when referring to the religious movement.

Spiritualism in Europe and South America

In France, Baron Du Potet was fascinated by spiritualist phenomena, as he had been for years with mesmerism. He published his *Journal du Magnétisme,* which covered twelve years of his investigations, from 1836 to 1848. In this journal he spoke of direct voice trance speaking, levitation, clairvoyance, materializations, apports, healing and many other phenomena. Another Baron, Baron Guldenstubbe, was the man who introduced table tipping to France, from the United States. This became a craze which swept into England. It is still very much practiced today.

In Italy the most striking medium was Eusapia Palladino (1854-1918); in many ways as spectacular as D. D. Home. In later years she was, on several occasions, caught out as a fraud, but these few instances could never eclipse the vast majority of her séances undertaken in the most rigid of investigative circumstances, totally precluding falsity.

She never managed levitation on the scale of Home's window-to-window maneuver, but levitation of objects she did do. One such event occurred at a sitting with Camille Flammarion and Guillaume de Fontenay. Before the séance Flammarion made a detailed investigation of the room. He checked windows and doors, curtains and drapes, chairs, the sofa; everything. He looked for electrical wires, batteries, any form of concealed mechanism, but found nothing. Madame Zelma Blech, the hostess, stripped and searched the medium but found nothing suspicious. The sitting then took place in full light and is comprehensively described by Flammarion (in *Mysterious Psychic Forces,* London 1907):

The medium sits before the curtain, turning her back to it. A table is placed before her — a kitchen table, made of spruce, weighing about fifteen pounds. I examined this table and found nothing in it suspicious. It could be moved about in every direction.

I sit at first on the left of Eusapia, then on her right side. I make sure as far as possible of her hands, and her feet, by personal control. Thus, for example, to begin with, in order to be sure that she should not lift the table either by her hands or her legs, or her feet, I take her left hand in my left hand, I place my right open hand upon her knees, and I place my right foot upon her left foot. Facing me, M. Guillaume de Fontenay, no more disposed than I to be duped, takes charge of her right hand and her right foot.

There is full light . . . At the end of three minutes the table begins to move, balancing itself, and rising sometimes to the right, sometimes to the left. A minute afterwards it is lifted to a height of about nine inches, and remains there two seconds.

In a second trial, I take the two hands of Eusapia in mine. A notable levitation is produced, nearly under the same conditions. We repeat the same experiments thrice, in such a way that five levitations of the table take place in a quarter of an hour, and for several seconds the four feet are completely lifted from the floor, to the height of about nine inches.

Another Frenchman, Hypolyte Leon Denizard Rivail (1804-1869), was told by a medium that in one of his previous incarnations his name had been Allan. A second medium said that in another lifetime it had been

Kardec (or Kardek). Rivail therefore adopted the name "Allan Kardec" and as such became the father of "Spiritism." Spiritism is the term used for the popular form of spiritualism found in both France and South America.

Kardec worked with a number of early mediums, and through them accumulated a vast amount of information relating to the progress of the human spirit. Foremost in that information was the belief in reincarnation, something not necessarily accepted by all spiritualists in either England or America.

The medium Kardec worked with was Celina Bequet (also known as Celina Japhet). Celina channeled information from both her grandfather and from Anton Mesmer, and gave out medical advice.

Kardec organized the mass of material obtained through Celina and, without mentioning her name, published much of it under the title *Le Livre des Esprits* ("The Spirits' Book"). Eight years later, in 1864, he published *Le Livre des Mediums* ("The Mediums' Book"), which included most of the balance of Celina's material.

Kardec's form of "Spiritism" was picked up from his writings in South America — most notably in Brazil — where it is also known as *Kardecism*. One of the tenets put forward by Kardec was that charity was essential for salvation and the greatest act of charity is to bestow health. From this, psychic healing developed and grew to where Brazil became one of the most active countries practicing it today. There are many Brazilian Spiritist hospitals where medical doctors work side by side with mediums. In 1925, Jeronimo Candido Gomide founded a Spiritist community — the only one of its kind in the world — where the mentally ill could be treated. Today Palmelo has over two thousand inhabitants, including a large number of mental patients.

Another form of South American Spiritism is
Umbanda; a cross between spiritualism and Voodoo. It is
similar to the practice of *Candomblé,* found in Bahiá and
Recife. In Umbanda the priestess, acting as a medium, is
known as a *cavalo,* or "horse." She is only permitted to
invoke disembodied spirits. The rites can take place
almost anywhere out in the open, but it is preferred that
they be close to water. In Candomblé the medium may
only invoke "nature spirits," for it is believed that to
bring the shades of the dead could cause "remnants of
the suffering world" to return also.

In Voodoo itself is found a ritual which is almost
totally spiritualistic in nature, even to the extent that the
priestess plays the part of a medium. I described it in my
book *Anatomy of the Occult* (Samuel Weiser, New York
1977):

> *(This Haitian ritual) is called "Retrait de l'esprit de
> l'eau" (Return of the spirits from beneath the
> water). A small canvas, tent-like enclosure is erected
> in the hounfor. Inside are placed various small
> offerings together with a tub of water and a stool for
> the "Mambo" (Priestess) to sit on. The Mambo
> enters and the entrance-flap is closed and secured
> after her. Several "hounsi" (initiates) then sit or lie
> on the ground before the structure, each holding a
> "govi" (the earthenware jars which house the spirits
> of the dead). As the people gather around, the
> Mambo can be heard chanting in "langage," a
> secret ritual language. There is a litany as she calls
> on the "loa" (gods), and the people respond. This
> may last for a half-hour or more. Eventually, how-
> ever, there is silence.*

A sharp cry from the Mambo is the signal for the first hounsi to slip her govi under the canvas into the tent. After a moment the sound of rushing water is heard, soon followed by a strained, rather hoarse, voice. The voice will call the name of one of those crowded around the tent. It is invariably recognized as being the voice of a dead relative. A conversation between the two will ensue, sometimes with the Mambo putting in a word here and there. It is not unknown for the Mambo to be speaking when the dead ancestor is speaking.

The ancestor may be consulted on family matters; his advice may be asked on a variety of things. He, or she, may have some vital message to impart. At one such séance that I witnessed, the voice of a recently deceased man informed his daughter that a neighbor had borrowed a sum of money just prior to the father's death. No one else knew of the loan so, at the death, the neighbor had kept quiet thinking he would never have to repay it. He little thought of his lender returning from the grave to demand repayment to his daughter!

All the while the voices are speaking there is heard the rushing of waters in the background. Although the Mambo has a bowl of water in the enclosure with her, this background noise is not one that can be reproduced using that bowl . . . When the voice has been heard the govi is returned, under the flap, to the hounsi and the next jar taken in.

Interestingly this is, in its turn, very similar to the Yuwipi Vision Talk Ceremony of the Oglala Sioux Amerindians. The shamanic Yuwipi refers to himself as *Tunkasila,* meaning "interpreter" or "medium." In the

sweat lodge he simply speaks with the spirits and tells the
others what they say. But in the Vision Talk Ceremony,
the Yuwipi is covered with a cloth and securely bound.
All light is extinguished and then the singers start their
songs. In the darkness the various sacred rattles are
heard. The clatter of them resounds around the black-
ened room, as they strike against the walls, ceiling and
floor. Then small sparks are seen as they sound, as
though the rattles were metal striking against flint.
These sparks signal the arrival of the spirits — spirits in
the sense of an ancient race of pygmy-like warriors — to
whom the Yuwipi speaks. There is more singing and
dancing by the participants. This leads to a healing for
those in the hut who need it. Those being healed often
will hear the spirits speaking directly to them; whispering into their ear as the healing progresses. They may
even feel the spirits touch them. As the ceremony fin-
ishes, the lights are brought back and the Yuwipi is
found kneeling in his inner sacred circle, the cloth that
had covered him folded neatly beside him and the cord
rolled up and lying on top of it.

Voodoo Worshipper, Possessed by the Loa, is Interrogated

V

PREPARATION FOR MEDIUMSHIP

Question Yourself

As stated in Chapter One, a medium is a connecting link between this physical world and the world of spirit. Anyone can learn to act as that link; anyone can become a medium.

How sincere are you in your desire to become a medium? This is something serious and should not be undertaken lightly. Do you want to channel for some reason of ego, or will you be doing it in a serious and dedicated manner, genuinely desiring positive results for the good of all concerned? It seems that those who do not have the true desire and the *belief* that it can be done, have a much harder time of it than others. To try it "just to see if it works" will not bring the same results as trying it in the sure knowledge that it can be done. There *must* be a knowledge that this is possible.

Start off by acknowledging to yourself that you do have a belief in the afterlife; that you do know that our spirits live on at another, higher, level of existence after physical death. For without this belief, you are certainly not going to get far in your attempts at development. Then, having acknowledged this belief, one of the first steps is to ask yourself the questions "Do I really want to become a medium?" and, if so, "*Why* do I want to become a medium?"

Is it simply to prove to yourself that there is a life after death, or to prove that to others? Is it a desire to communicate with specific departed loved ones? If so, then perhaps you can do so without actually becoming a medium yourself.

But perhaps there is more of the lure of achieving fame and fortune; of flaunting your psychic abilities? Or perhaps there is just a desire to continue developing psychic abilities that have already shown themselves? There are many possible answers to "Why do I want to become a medium?" and no single one of them is necessarily the right one. Conversely, none of them may be really "wrong." (Certainly many mediums in the past have achieved both fame and fortune. Some have certainly flaunted their abilities. Whether or not this is "approved" by others is something else and, perhaps, a moot point.)

To begin, you have to know yourself. Who are you? What is your purpose in life? What path is it that you wish to tread and where, exactly, does that path lead? Do you have goals — both long term and short term? It is a good idea to sit down with a piece of paper and a pencil and address some of these questions. Ask yourself these, and similar ones, in all sincerity, and see what you come up with.

Know, too, that not all people work the same way. We are all individuals; we all develop differently, even on psychic levels. What works for one person may not work for another, so some experimentation may well be necessary. We also develop at different rates; some become strong channels in a very short time, while others work for years to achieve that same state. No one can guarantee that you will become a medium of any particular type within a certain specified period of time.

Ivy Northage, the celebrated English medium, said:

Mediumship on its highest level is a vocation. It is a surrendering of oneself to the influences of the spirit world to form a bridge by which help and support can be given to those who are seeking it. If I had to compile a golden rule for its development, I would place first on my list "The less of me, the more of spirit, the better medium I will become" . . . all that spirit really requires from us is a telephone; a means by which they can use our psychic equipment.

—*Mediumship Made Simple*,
Psychic Press Ltd., London 1986

Many teachers urge that our motives for spiritual development should be of the highest, and that we must avoid getting carried away by our own sense of importance.

Affirmations

Affirmations are a good start and lead in to more direct development. Indeed, affirmations can remain a very useful tool throughout your development and long after your psychic maturity.

Affirmations are positive statements repeated by an individual, thereby establishing them in the subconscious mind and reinforcing the conscious mind. In other words, to repeat several times over, every morning, that you are (for example) growing more attractive and self-assured will actually work on your inner self to the point where not only will you sincerely believe that you are becoming more attractive and self-assured, but you actually will become more attractive and self-assured.

Affirmations can be composed for just about anything and are especially effective for psychic development. As Stuart Wilde says (*Affirmations*, Taos, New Mexico 1987):

> *An Affirmation of word will serve for almost anything — health, wealth, happiness — whatever you are concentrating on at the time.*

Wilde goes on to say that the affirmations you compose yourself are by far the most effective, and this is true. But to give you an idea of the type of composition, here are one or two you might use for starting mediumship. Write some more of your own.

> *"Psychic powers are natural powers and I possess them strongly."*

> *"My natural psychic abilities are opening up and flowing."*

> *"By believing in my psychic power I unveil my natural mediumship."*

> *"Every day, in every way, my mediumship develops and progresses."*

> *"The gateway to the world of spirit swings open wide for me."*

It can be seen that affirmations can be slanted in any direction, depending on where you feel your greatest need(s) might be. You can take any affirmation — or two, or three (don't take too many though; you'll dilute your concentration) — and repeat it several times every day. A lot of people write it out and then post it up about their house/apartment. To get up in the morning and see your affirmation in front of you, stuck on the bathroom mirror, prompts you to say it there and then. On the refrigerator door is another good place.

Post them all over the place. Write them on colorful, eye-catching paper, or with brightly-colored inks. Say them and get into the habit of saying them. Say them . . . and *believe them!*

Meditation

Next to the belief that it is possible, relaxation is the key to making contact with the world of spirit. You will get nowhere if you are tense. Practice relaxation by way of meditation. Properly used, meditation can open the door to individual growth and personal advancement. Yet it is a practice that is simplicity itself.

There are many different ways to meditate. Transcendental Meditation has been very popular in the past and is still used by many. Edgar Cayce's is another common method. There are a number of variations on the theme. Once again there is no one right way; find what is right for you. Here is my own method; one you might try.

First of all you must feel comfortable and secure. Wear loose, comfortable clothing — just slipping on a robe when you first get up in the morning, before you dress, and going straight to your meditation can be a good idea. Meditate somewhere where you know you will not be interrupted; where you can sit quietly for ten or fifteen minutes without being disturbed. Disconnect the telephone, make sure there is no television or radio noise, and lock the door.

Sit in a comfortable chair which has a straight back and armrests. Sit with your feet flat on the floor and your arms on the armrests. Be able to sit there for about fifteen minutes without discomfort. Early morning or late evening are good times for meditating. Not only is exterior noise likely to be less but the general "vibes" of the atmosphere are more conducive to relaxation. Whenever you do it, try to always meditate at about the same time each day. Just once a day will do; twice a day (morning and evening) is better.

Start to relax your body by doing a few headrolls. Close your eyes and let your head come forward on your chest. Start to roll it around: up onto your right shoulder, to the back, around to the left shoulder and back to where you started, down in front. Roll it around three times and then reverse the process and go back around three times the other way.

Now bring your head back upright and hunch up your shoulders; up as close as you can get them to your ears. Hold them there for a moment, then let them relax and drop. Do this three times.

Take three good, deep breaths. Really fill your lungs as you inhale, and then squeeze out every last little bit of air as you exhale. (Some people like to visualize themselves breathing in white, positive light and then breathing out all negativity.)

Now, breathing normally, concentrate on relaxing your body, taking it through a bit at a time from toes to head. Focus your attention on your toes and feel them relaxing. Feel tension going out of them; any little aches and pains disappearing. Continue through to your feet as a whole — the balls of the feet, the soles, the heels, the ankles. You make it happen that they relax. *Feel* them relax. Then take that relaxation up to your calves. Feel those calf muscles relaxing! Move on to the knees.

Continue in this fashion throughout the entire body: thighs and upper legs, groin, buttocks, hips, spine, stomach, back, chest, shoulders, fingers, hands, wrists, lower and upper arms, neck, throat, chin, jaw, eyes, cranial area, ears, scalp . . . relax every muscle, vein, nerve and fiber. If you are familiar with hypnosis you may recognize this as an induction technique. It is very effective (and can be used, as will be seen later, for bringing on mediumistic trance).

When you have relaxed in this fashion you can simply sit there and enjoy it, or you can go on to do other psychic work. In Transcendental Meditation you would concentrate on a mantra — a short word or phrase (more just a sound than an actual word) to keep any thoughts from intruding as you sit and relax. But meditation is an excellent time to permit entry of certain things. Ignore mundane thoughts — "Oh boy! When I've finished here I've got to go out and mow the lawn!" or "The rent is due tomorrow and I haven't got the money!" Try, as much as possible, to think of nothing in particular. This is not easy but it can be done, and is the reason for the TM mantra. The trouble with something like a mantra is that it keeps out the worthwhile along with the mundane. Often it is in meditation that you get your first contact with spirit, or with your Spirit Guide. In Chapter Seven I will give a guided meditation that will bring you into contact with your Spirit Guide(s). For now, however, just use meditation as a tool for learning to relax totally and completely. If something should come, just accept it but don't dwell on it. Simply try to keep your mind as blank as possible.

Your conscious mind is like a spoiled child, it is constantly demanding attention. But it can be disciplined. It can be taught to sit quietly and wait. Once this happens you will start to get positive results. Sit in meditation and relax. Enjoy it. Ten minutes is probably enough time to start. You can gradually increase this to fifteen or even twenty minutes, if you wish.

Meditation

At the end of your meditation period, reverse your relaxation technique: go through your body from the top of your head down to your toes. This time, however, feel your muscles awakening, feeling fresh and energized, ready for anything you want to tackle. Finish up by opening your eyes and, after a couple of minutes of reorientation, standing up. You should feel great!

Safeguards

"Like attracts like" is the adage, and it has proven to be true. For this reason you really need have no fear of attracting evil entities of any sort to you while practicing your mediumship.

Yet this is certainly a common fear among newcomers to spiritualistic phenomena. Indiscriminate use of items like Ouija boards has brought problems to some people in the past, which has helped give rise to this apprehension. But, as I say, *like attracts like.* In other words, if you are the sort of person who is positive, seeking to help others through your mediumship and looking to advance spiritually, then you will attract nothing but good to you. You really have nothing to fear. On the other hand, if you are the sort who takes delight in playing pranks with a sadistic twist to them, are not averse to swindling people out of their savings and wouldn't think twice about dealing in stolen goods, then you might well draw similar spirits to you. And along with such negative spirits you might well attract negative "entities," for want of a better term; elemental beings from other realms who might be looking for a means of entry into this one. Ivy Northage (previously quoted) says:

> *I am often asked if psychic activity invites evil spirits. Accepting a reasonable and sensible approach to all such phenomena, the answer is a positive no. Like attracts like, and someone sincerely desirous of developing their gifts for the good of humanity cannot be in touch with evil. It should be remembered, however, that psychic ability on the astral level is as a light in a foggy street. Therefore, uncontrolled or denied the spiritual stimulus of upliftment afforded by the guides, it can expose you to mischievous or lost*

*spirits which, once attached, can be difficult to dis-
lodge without firm refusal of psychic activity on the
part of the medium.*

With all this in mind it behooves the sensible
medium always to take some precautions *just in case.* It
takes but a moment to erect a psychic barrier around
you, so why not do so every time you prepare to do any
sort of psychic work? And there I would even include
meditation, as I spoke about it above. Here is a simple little cleansing and protection process you can go through
right before you meditate, right before you try table tipping, psychometry, automatic writing or a full-blown
séance. In other words, every time.

Sit quietly for a moment, eyes closed, feet flat on
the floor, hands loosely in your lap or on the arms of
your chair. Breathe deeply and evenly and calm yourself.
Then, as you breathe, imagine that with each intake of
breath you are drawing into your body the soft, positive,
blue light of protection; as you breathe out you are pushing out all negativity. Feel this blue light (some people
prefer to "see" a white light or a golden one; use
whichever color you feel most comfortable with) coming
up into your body through your feet. Feel and sense that
it is coming up from "Mother Earth;" from the great
goodness of Nature. Even if you are sitting in a room several floors up in a building, you can still sense this energy
coming up out of the ground and then slowly climbing
up through the building until it reaches your floor and
your feet. Look upon this as an attunement with Nature
and with all the positive aspects of the myriad forms of
life in and on the earth.

As you breathe in and out, feel/sense your body filling with this positiveness and driving out all the negativity until you are completely filled with good energy.
Then keep going for awhile.

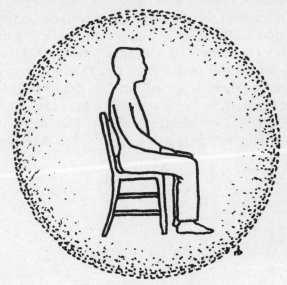

Protective Psychic Shell

"See" the light expanding until you are totally enclosed in a sphere of it; a ball of light with you in its center. This is your protective shell. This is the egg of which you are the yolk. Nothing negative can break through it. Know this and accept it. It will serve and protect you.

If you are of an especially religious turn you might want to add the saying of a prayer, such as "The Lord's Prayer," to this practice. You can do this as you work on the power/light building. Another alternative is to see white, gold, blue, or whatever color light descending from "above" (from God/Goddess/All That Is) and entering your body at the crown of the head or the position of the Third Eye (see Chapter Sixteen on chakras) rather than coming up from the ground.

Do not hesitate to do anything that will give you an added sense of security and protection. But at the same time don't, please, scare yourself into believing that you are about to embark on a perilous journey that is fraught with danger and from which you may not return! As I said earlier, there is probably no need for this protective measure at all; we are just doing it to err on the side of safety. So do it as a matter of course, then carry on without thinking anything more about it. You'll be fine.

VI

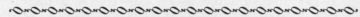

DIFFICULTIES OF SPIRIT COMMUNICATION

The Problem of Connecting

One of the questions often raised at the idea of spirit communication is, if it is truly possible, why aren't many more people doing it? Also, of the millions of people who die, why don't more come back through mediums? The short answer to both these questions is that really good communicators are comparatively rare. If there were a lot of good mediums then many more people would be able to "come back" from the spirit world and many more potential mediums would be encouraged to develop.

In order to communicate you need both a "sender" who wants to communicate, together with a "receiver" who is also trying to make contact at that same time. Plus, you must have the medium of communication — the person who is able to make the connection. A good simile might be to imagine a host of people in the United States wanting to speak to relatives in Europe, but with an extremely limited supply of telephone operators, no known phone numbers, and the relatives in Europe unaware that they are trying to be contacted!

To continue the simile, when a connection is made, there might very well be a bad line, and the operator may be unable to make a direct connection and have to relay everything back and forth . . . with the attendant problems of interpretation!

In the "here and now" it is not always easy to understand what someone is trying to say to you. In everyday life there is constant misunderstanding and misinterpretation. "What do you mean?" "What are you trying to say?" These are not uncommon expressions in the course of many "normal" conversations. Just listen to any conversation between a parent and a child — especially a teenager — and you'll see what I mean! It should not come as a surprise, then, to find that communication with the spirit world can be even more difficult.

In the past there were many more mediums though, even then, really good mediums were never plentiful. In the earliest days of the spiritualist movement, and the development of the Spiritualist Church, there were a lot of "home development circles." These were gatherings of people all equally interested in spiritualism and all eager to develop their gifts of mediumship. With the advent of television and the development of radio and the movies, among other things, development circles quickly became a thing of the past. Today, therefore — especially with the added distractions of home computers, Nintendo games, outdoor sports of an incredible variety, ease of travel, etc. — there are very few mediums with only a trickle under development. Yet to make contact with spirits of the dead and to learn of the afterlife must surely be far more exciting than any television program!

Atmospherics

One of the difficulties that is often mentioned by spirits when they first make contact is that they become easily fatigued. They seem quickly to become exhausted and complain of feelings of suffocation, necessitating breaking the connection for a short time. They will then later return, apparently refreshed. The reason for the fatigue is unknown, though some have suggested it has to do with the density of the medium's aura. Obviously there is a very delicate "attunement" that takes place between the spirit and the medium to bring about successful communication.

Another reason for difficult communication with direct voice, automatic writing and the like, is simply that the spirit is unused to the medium's body. All of us have certain mental and physical habits which we form, making it easier for us to do certain things in certain ways peculiar to us. If you were suddenly transplanted into someone else's body (especially someone of the opposite sex) you might well experience great difficulty trying to do the simplest things. So it is with spirit trying to use the medium's body. Just trying to adjust to the medium's vocal cords can take a while, let alone trying to use his or her finger, hand and wrist muscles to hold a pencil and write.

Dates, Names and Ideas

There are other difficulties of communication, other than just those of the mechanics of making the connection. For example, if a spirit is giving a message which is being received clairvoyantly or clairsentiently, the medium can frequently pick up the general idea of the message without necessarily getting the exact wording. Yet if all that is being relayed is a name or a date, or some other abstract, there is no general "idea" that can be grasped. A spirit may be able to convey the feelings of love felt for the person with whom they are communicating, and this may be picked up and passed on by the medium. Or the word "table" will evince a particular picture in the mind of the medium. But how does one pick up the "feelings" of, say, *May 27, 1963,* or of *Fred?* This is one of the reasons why mediums who seem otherwise excellent may fall down on receiving accurate names, numbers, dates, etc.

Where dates are concerned there is the added factor that time, as we know it, is not a part of the world of spirit. Time is human-made. It is a convenience only (or inconvenience!).

Have you ever been away on vacation; perhaps just relaxing in the mountains or at the beach, and then suddenly had the thought "Hey! What day is it today?" With no need to keep note of the passing of time, with no pressing appointments to make or keep, it is easy to lose track of how many hours, days, or even weeks have gone by. And, to continue the idea of not having to make and keep appointments, why should you bother to keep track of how many hours, days, or weeks have gone by? No reason at all!

So it may well be in the world of spirit. You can be where you want to be whenever you want to be; you can be with whomever you want whenever you want to be. Would it be any wonder that you would lose track of the passing of time, as it is recorded back here on earth?

Symbolism and Its Interpretation

A symbol is a sign; an expression to give the impression of something else. As Webster puts it, "Something concrete that represents or suggests another thing that cannot in itself be represented or visualized."

The only drawback with symbols is that they have to be interpreted. Certain symbols have become universal and are immediately recognized as representing specific things — traffic signs are a good example of this symbolism — whereas others are so infrequently used or so personal that someone unfamiliar with them would have a hard time interpreting them. This can often be the case in mediumship; something is presented in the form of a symbol which the medium may or may not correctly interpret.

Don't forget that we never actually see anything in the physical world as it really is! What we do is to realize, through our five senses, various aspects or qualities of the object. For example, if you are looking at an orange, your sense of sight tells you that it is a reddish-yellow sphere with an irregular, pock-marked surface. Your sense of touch tells you that it is round, smooth yet slightly rough, and cool. Your sense of smell supplies you with the information that it has a distinctive yet pleasant odor, which is confirmed by your sense of taste. In this particular instance your sense of hearing does not enter into it.

Now all these things which appeal to your senses are "qualities" of the orange rather than being the orange itself. The orange is always something different from all of these, and above and beyond them, and is more inclusive than any of these qualities and symbols.

So suppose you were to take away one of those symbols — the color, for example. The orange would immediately become invisible to you, and yet it would continue to exist. This shows that the symbols are very inadequate and imperfect representations of a vaster "something" lying behind them. They represent only a small fraction of the totality of the thing as it really exists.

Interpreting Actions

Interpreting actions seen clairvoyantly can especially become a problem in mediumship. When we communicate with one another on the physical plane, we do so by a pre-arranged code. We either use written symbols or we go by our facial expressions, motions of the head and hands, together with vocal sounds. If we did not have these pre-arranged codes we would have great difficulty making ourselves understood. This can be seen when two people meet who do not speak the same language.

Suppose you want to tell a Russian, who speaks no English, to get something — let's say a watch — from another room. It would be useless to say the word "watch." You would probably tap your wrist, go through the motions of winding a watch, setting the hands, etc., then point to him and then to the other room. If he did not understand what you were trying to say you would have great difficulty getting what you wanted.

In *Amazing Secrets Of the Psychic World* (New York 1975), I give an example of what might happen with a medium trying to interpret the actions of a spirit seen through clairvoyance:

> *He taps his stomach and looks at a spot over his left side. He seems to wish to convey the impression that*

*he suffered much from bowel trouble, perhaps a can-
cer on the left side. Yes, he seems to be taking something away from the body; evidently they removed
some growth. Now he is examining his hand. He is
looking intently. Now he is doing something with his
fingers. I can't see what it is; a little movement. Was
he connected with machinery in life . . . ?*

In actual fact dear dead Uncle Charles was trying to
let you know that it really was him there by doing what
he had always done, so many times, while alive: he had a
favorite pocket watch which he would take out of his vest
pocket, wind, and reset if necessary! He never had any
stomach problems, cancer, or connection with machinery. So here, although the medium had made contact
and had correctly seen Uncle Charles' actions, he had
incorrectly interpreted what was seen to the point where
the recipient could not believe there had even been any
true contact!

This is a not uncommon problem. The answer to all
this is simply, as a medium, to not interpret what you see;
just describe it exactly as you see it and leave the actual
interpretation to the sitter.

Triviality in Messages

A criticism often leveled at spiritualism is that the messages received from the spirits are so many times so trivial. "Why don't they tell you something important?"
"Why are they wasting time talking about an incident in
your childhood?" "Why don't they tell you what's coming
up in the future?"

In fact it is the very triviality of most messages that
underscores their authenticity. If I were sitting with a

medium and she (or he) claimed to have my grandfather come through, it would leave me quite cold to be told that he saw me becoming rich and famous. It would be nice to hear, perhaps, but I could hear the same thing from a carnival fortuneteller. How much more striking to be told that he was reminding me of a certain time when, as a child, I accompanied him to the banks of the River Thames and to tell me of what happened when we stood watching another young boy fishing. A "trivial" incident, yes. But an absolute confirmation that I was indeed in contact with my late grandfather.

Many, if not most, people sitting with mediums are doing so because they are looking for the comfort of knowing that there is a life after death and that their loved ones are still available to them. The so-called trivial details are the ones which give this assurance more than could anything else.

If you are a regular sitter, then you can go on beyond the trivia stage, by all means. And most people do. It is, however, the trivia that critics seem to dwell on, perhaps feeling that it makes spiritualism an easy mark.

Names, Colors and Lights

As I have mentioned, names are not easy to get across. Family names, however, can often be projected through symbolism. For example, if a medium describes an elderly man and then says something like, "He is showing me a field . . . a large green field . . . and now an inn. A field and an inn." The sitter might well immediately recognize that the spirit was giving the name "Fielding," a name well known to the sitter. A man sitting sewing could be representative of the name "Taylor," and so on.

There are many names that can be got across through this kind of symbolism. As a medium you need to be aware that this may be the sort of information that is being channeled.

There are also symbols that have almost become the Universal Symbols of spiritualistic communication. They include the following:

Bells: wedding; celebration.

Black border: as on a letter, indicates a loss.

Clouds: if white, happiness; dark, misfortune; receding and fading away, indicates a journey.

Colors: these have various meanings, basically whatever you "feel" they mean to you (and you should here be consistent). Generally blue, lilac and purple are associated with spirituality; red with passion and/or anger; yellow/orange with change; pink with love and health; green with money.

Key: success.

Letter: news coming.

Light: specks of light show good progress in spiritual and psychic development. A bright light is often a spirit trying to communicate.

There may be use of any number of symbols that become your own personal ones. For example, you may always see a large U-Haul whenever any sitter is going to relocate, or an airplane when they are to take a trip. Over the years you will come to recognize when a particular thing is a symbol rather than something integral to the specific sitter.

VII

~o~o~o~o~o~o~o~o~o~o~o~o~o~o~o~o~o~

SPIRIT GUIDES

Spirit Guides and Guardian Angels

The belief that human beings have spirit guardians
watching over them is found in many ages and many soci-
eties around the world. The ancient Greeks, Romans,
Egyptians, the Chinese, African tribes, Amerindians, in
the Old Testament and New, in Mohammedan belief —
everywhere is found one or another aspect of this belief.

Spiritualism certainly agrees that we each have a
spirit guide. It is not someone we choose; they choose us.
Also, you may have more than one. Some mediums find
they have one guide who works with them in clairvoyance, for example, and another who works with them to
do automatic writing, or physical mediumship. There are
some mediums who specialize in psychic healing (see
Chapter Sixteen) and have a whole group of guides,
some or all of whom were doctors in their earthly lives.
(Not that all guides were, necessarily, once on this plane.
There are some who have never manifested here.) It is
also possible, incidentally, for a guide to work with more
than one medium.

One point to keep in mind is that your importance
does not increase in proportion to the number of guides
you have! If you hear a medium constantly speaking

about her large number of guides, it may just be her ego she is stroking. You can be just as good a medium — probably better — with only one guide.

If your guide gives you details of his or her previous life/lives on the physical plane, accept it as something interesting but don't dwell on it. It is only natural that you should look for some personal details of your guide's previous existence, but to get too caught up in what they did, where they lived, etc., is to detract from your main purpose, which is to do the work you have chosen to do.

The Doorkeeper

The term "Doorkeeper" is often given to the one guide who works most closely with you in mediumship. He or she is the one who organizes the spirits on the Second Level, ready to come through you to the sitters on this level. He will ensure that the spirits are there and will help them, if necessary. He will also keep away any unwanted spirits, should any unsavory types be attracted for whatever reason. The late medium Ena Twigg's personal guide and doorkeeper was "Philip;" Estelle Roberts' was "Red Cloud;" Arthur Ford had "Fletcher," Ivy Northage has "Chan," and William Rainen "Dr. Peebles." (Not every medium is necessarily aware of his or her doorkeeper, however. The New York medium George Anderson does not mention one, neither does San Diego's Chris Meredith.)

Ivy Northage (*Mediumship Made Simple*) says:

> *The whole area of spiritual service is governed by vibrations. The guides are responsible for harmonising these vibrations with a medium, communicating spirit, and recipient. This trinity remains*

unchanged whatever expression of mediumship is used. The doorkeeper controls the motivation of these vibrations to the varying degree the spiritual service demands . . .

No guide can use the sensitive without his assurance that harmonious vibrations can be maintained . . . While all spiritual service is co-ordinated with the guides, they cannot continue with any effort without his permission. His responsibility, however, like the guide's, ends with legitimate spiritual activity.

Free Will

We all have free will, so our guides do not interfere with the way we live our lives. That doesn't mean to say that they would not try to influence you if they saw you seemingly bent on self-destruction. I'm sure they would. But any such interference would always be by suggestion — usually subtle — so that the last word is definitely yours.

Another name sometimes used for a guide is a "spirit control," though this is more of a misnomer since, as I say, they do guide rather than control you. Another term occasionally used is "spirit associate."

Your guide would never lead you astray, or cause you to do anything negative or destructive. If ever you feel you are getting those sort of directions, stop and question just where they might be coming from.

Finding Your Spirit Guide

We all have a spirit guide, whether we are aware of it or not. Many Christians think in terms of a "Guardian Angel," perhaps even identifying it with one of the Christian angels or archangels, or one of the Saints, and can accept the concept in those terms.

As a spiritualist and potential medium, it is a good idea to make contact with your guide. There is an easy way to do this, which is through a meditation journey.

Begin as I detailed in Chapter Five: make sure you are quite secure (unlikely to be interrupted) and sit in your meditation chair. You will be going through the relaxation technique I gave you and then going on from there, on a psychic journey. There are two main ways you can take this journey. You can carefully read through what follows and get it firmly in your mind, then you can repeat it to yourself (it doesn't have to be word-for-word; just get the general feel of it) and follow through with the suggestions as you give them to yourself. Or you can first read the journey onto a tape recorder and then, when you are ready, simply play it back and follow through on the suggestions. Either way can be effective. The choice is yours.

❦❦❦❦

You are walking along a country lane. The sun is shining down and you feel warm and happy. There is an open field on your left and a large wood on your right. You can hear birds singing in the trees and a gentle breeze wafts against your face.

You see, ahead of you, a small path that leads off to the right, into the wood. Take that path. It leads at a slight downward angle, winding in amongst the trees. You can see the sun up above, shining down through the branches and creating a wonderfully warm and comforting environment. Small animals, such as squirrels, rabbits and chipmunks, peek out at you as you go on your way. You catch an occasional glimpse of a baby deer through the trees.

The angle of descent gradually steepens, and you come to a cliff edge. You are not very high up; in fact, no higher than the tops of the trees on the ground below the cliff. You see that someone has cut large steps into the face of the cliff and these lead down to the wooded ground below. You go down these steps. It is an easy descent and you feel safe and secure as you descend. At the bottom you cross the short expanse of grass to go, once more, in amongst the trees.

As you move on, you soon become aware of the babbling of a brook. The sound gets louder as you approach it. As the path makes a turn to the right, you see the brook ahead of you; its busy waters rushing over and around small and large stones. The path you are on follows along the side of the brook and you carry on along it, noticing how the water swirls and eddies as it goes on its journey. Other small streams come in to join it and gradually it swells until it becomes a small river. As you walk on, beside it, you enjoy occasional glimpses of fish in the river, and of a duck or two that lands on the water then takes off again.

A large tree has fallen and stretches across the river, its upper branches on the far bank. Take the opportunity to cross over; jump up onto the tree trunk and walk across. You feel firm and secure, knowing you will not slip or fall.

On the other side, you notice a large number of wild flowers growing in amongst the trees and underbrush. There is another path — you were obviously not the first to cross by the fallen tree. Follow along the path and notice the flowers, and again, the animals and birds.

Ahead of you the trees start to thin and you come out in a field. Stop and stand with the wood behind you. Fields stretch away to the horizon ahead of you. Off to the left you can make out high mountains, and to the right you can see the wood curving around and off with more fields beyond. But in front of you, in the middle of the field at whose edge you stand, there is a circle of standing stones. Each stone stands nine or ten feet tall. There are a number of them forming this circle. Great granite monoliths. They look older than time; as if they have stood here for century upon century. Count how many there are.

Move forward into the ring. You feel happy, warm and comforted, as though the stones are guardians surrounding you and keeping out all negativity. Walk into the very center of the circle they form and sit down on the grass. You are aware of the warmth of the sun and the sound of the birds. Again you feel that gentle breeze on your cheeks. Close your eyes for a moment and breathe deeply. Breathe in the wonderful, positive energies of that sacred place.

As you sit there quietly, you become aware of another person joining you. This person has come up from behind you and now moves around to face you. It is a good presence; a comforting one. It is your Personal Guide. It is the Doorkeeper who has watched over your progress for many years. Don't yet open your eyes, but stand up and reach out your hands and take those that are offered. Feel them. Feel the warmth and love that comes from them.

Now open your eyes and see your guide. Is it a man or a woman? Does it appear young or old? What is it wearing? Notice everything about this guide. Ask by what name you should call him or her and greet them appropriately. Ask if they have any special message for you.

Know that this stone circle is your "Special Place." You can come here at any time, knowing that you can here meet with your guide, or anyone else you wish, and be perfectly safe and secure. You can here ask all you wish to know of your guide. No one else can come here without your permission.

When you have finished speaking with your guide, bid him or her goodbye and say that you will meet again very soon. Then turn and walk out of the circle, back towards the woods.

Retrace your steps, going back to the river and across the fallen tree trunk. Follow back along the path till it parts company with the stream. Go up the steps in the cliff and head out of the wood again, back onto the country road. Know that you have had a unique journey, but that you can repeat it any time you wish.

Find yourself back in your meditation chair, breath deeply and relax as you prepare to come back to your normal surroundings. Follow the steps I gave you in Chapter Five, for coming out of meditation, open your eyes and feel good!

❧❧❧❧

As I have said, you can return to your special place at any time you wish. If you wish to go straight there from entering meditation, without going on the long journey through the woods, then you may do so, though I do recommend taking the "long scenic route" for the first few times at least. Also, if you would prefer a different destination — a different "Special Place" — then you can have it. I know of one person who ends up going into a cave to meet his guide. I know of another whose special place is high up in a room in an old stone tower, and one who meets her guide underneath a waterfall! If you prefer to be in a room in a house with relatively modern surroundings, that too is fine. Simply let your journey take you to where you would feel most comfortable. On coming out of the woods, you may see an old castle which you enter, or you may cross the field and go into a house and then to a particular room. Whatever is the most comfortable place for you is the right place. If it is to be furnished, then furnish it as you will.

Wherever you decide to go, after first accessing it ask yourself some questions. What were your feelings on various stages of the journey? What animals did you see, and did you have any special feelings about them? Was there more to be seen than given by me in the general directions for the journey? If so, what? How did you feel when you first became aware of your guide being there? What did his or her hands feel like? What did he or she look like? What was the name? Was there any message?

There are no right or wrong answers to these questions. Simply study the answers and see if they have special meaning to you.

Records

It is a good idea to keep a notebook or journal of your development. Note the dates and times that you meditate, when you journey, and the results of your journeys. When you start communicating with your guide on a regular basis, most people certainly keep a record of all that he or she tells you. Later, when you are acting as a medium, keep up this journal.

VIII

⟨⬦⟩⟨⬦⟩⟨⬦⟩⟨⬦⟩⟨⬦⟩⟨⬦⟩⟨⬦⟩⟨⬦⟩⟨⬦⟩⟨⬦⟩⟨⬦⟩⟨⬦⟩⟨⬦⟩⟨⬦⟩⟨⬦⟩⟨⬦⟩

TRANCE

Levels of Brainwave Activity

There are four different levels of brainwave activity that prescribe altered states of consciousness. These are designated *beta, alpha, theta* and *delta.* Normal wide-awake consciousness is the beta state, with brainwaves ranging from 14 to 27 cycles per second. The next level down is the alpha level, and this is characterized by brainwaves of 8 to 13 cycles per second. Below this is theta at 4 to 8 cycles per second, and delta operates at 0 to 4 cycles per second.

As I say, beta is our usual wide-awake mode, though during this mode we spend up to 75% of our consciousness monitoring physical functions. The next step down, alpha, is achieved in meditation; also when we are daydreaming and when in the *hypnagogic* state just prior to falling asleep at night, and the *hypnapompic* state just as we are coming out of sleep in the morning. This would be a "light trance" state.

The theta state is the equivalent of a light sleep, where we are generally unaware of what is going on around us. It is possible to achieve this state when in deep meditation. Delta, the deepest level, is where we are absolutely sound asleep, with no knowledge whatsoever of what is happening about us. It is the equivalent of somnambulism in hypnosis.

Spontaneous Trance

Many mediums go into trance intentionally or spontaneously. This might be just a light one or one of the deeper variety. In the lighter trance the medium invariably has full memory after the event of all that transpired. In the deeper states, the medium has no knowledge of what took place the whole time he or she was in the altered state.

Sometimes a medium is not even aware of being in trance, because it is such a light one. For example, most mediums and psychics would swear they are not entranced when doing something like psychometry or simple clairvoyance, yet they have invariably slipped from the beta state into the beginnings of alpha.

Although, as will be shown, mediumistic trance can be induced hypnotically, it is essentially different from plain hypnotic trance. When a hypnotist places a subject under hypnosis, that subject remains in rapport with the hypnotist, a living person. In a mediumistic trance the medium loses all contact with the living and attunes to the spiritual realm, to the point where it is almost as though the spirit guide is the "hypnotist."

Trance Experience

William Stainton Moses (1839-1892), the nineteenth century English medium and religious teacher, described the trance of D. D. Home, which he witnessed:

> *By degrees Mr. Home's hands and arms began to twitch and move involuntarily. I should say that he has been partly paralysed, drags one of his legs, moves with difficulty, stoops and can endure very little physical exertion. As he passed into the trance state he drew power from the circle by extending his arms to them and mesmerising himself. All these acts are involuntary. He gradually passed into the trance state, and rose from the table, erect and a different man from what he was. He walked firmly, dashed out his arms and legs with great power and passed round to Mr. Crookes.*

Mrs. Leonore Piper (1859-1950), the Boston medium, who has been described as "the foremost trance medium in the history of psychical research," (*Encyclopedia of Occultism and Parapsychology*, Leslie A. Shepard, Ed. New York 1973) described her own trance thus:

> *I feel as if something were passing over my brain, making it numb; a sensation similar to that experienced when I was etherised, only the unpleasant odour of the ether is absent. I feel a little cold, too, not very, just a little, as if a cold breeze passed over me, and people and objects become smaller until they finally disappear; then, I know nothing more until I wake up, when the first thing I am conscious of is a bright, a very bright light, and then darkness, such darkness. My hands and arms begin to tingle just as one's foot tingles after it has been "asleep," and I see,*

as if from a great distance, objects and people in the
room; but they are very small and very black.

Nandor Fodor reports that:

On awakening from trance Mrs. Piper often pro-
nounced names and fragments of sentences which
appeared to have been the last impressions on her
brain. After that she resumed the conversation at
the point where it was broken off before she fell into
trance.

In the earlier days of mediumship the act of going
into trance frequently seemed a painful one; mediums
would grimace and contort their faces and bodies, some
even tearing their hair! Thankfully the process today
seems much easier, with the medium slipping into
unconsciousness as one slips into sleep.

Return from Trance

There seems to be a consensus regarding the medium's
feelings on returning from trance. There is a general
feeling of sorrow at having to leave the spirit level and
return to the "ugliness" of the earth plane. Even on a
bright sunny day the medium may feel that he or she is
returning to somewhere dark and dingy. There have also
been occasional comments from some mediums about
coming back "on a silver cord" of the type familiar in
astral projection.

Ivy Northage says of trance work:

The medium's mind is taken over to a greater or
lesser degree by the controlling spirit. In my own case
this was a gradual process of complete withdrawal

*on my part and an increasing command on Chan's
(her spirit guide). Its purpose in psychic and spiritual terms is to extend the power of spiritual influence to reach and obtain more positive response in
communication with the other world. Many would-
be mediums believe trance work will automatically
separate them from subconscious interference, but
this is not so. Its first essential is a loose etheric body,
together with a mental confidence in their own purpose and the ability of the guides who work with
them. It is never a substitute for positive mediumship, but can reduce obstruction to spirit activity
by creating a real dependence upon the guide, thus
enabling him to work more freely. This must depend
upon the depth of trance and the ability of the
medium to control his own thoughts and emotions.*

Trance, in the spiritualistic sense is, then, the freeing of the spiritual perception; the freeing of those
faculties which belong to the spiritual being thereby
suspending the physical being. As the physical senses
become dormant there is a sinking sensation or,
depending on the individual, it can be a soaring sensation. But it is a sensation of freedom; of leaving the
earthly restrictions on the physical body. Most mediums
say that it helps to be working in a circle of like-minded
people. Whether or not they are all holding hands,
there is a concentration of energies that can be enormously beneficial to the medium in passing into trance
and establishing contact with the Second Level.

The Best Way to Enter Trance

Many would-be mediums will find that they can pass easily into trance from the meditative state. Indeed, if you follow the instructions I've already given (see Chapter Seven) for finding your spirit guide, you can simply continue from there, speaking with your guide and having him/her go immediately into contact with other spirits.

But it might be preferable to keep your Special Place as just that, a special place — where only those you invite may enter. So, having made contact with your guide and, over a number of get-togethers, having established a good rapport, you may go on to arranging with him/her to act as go-between in bringing those in the world of spirit through to you (or through you to others) whenever you desire. You may, of course, wish to arrange another "Special Place," or setting, always to be used for just this purpose. Your guide will then take the initiative. Should you want to go into trance for purposes of mediumship (and don't forget that trance is not necessary for all forms of mediumship), he/she will facilitate the inducement and will be ready and waiting for you on the other side.

But many mediums have started their mediumship by having their trance induced by a second party; a hypnotist. As you read in Chapter Three, Andrew Jackson Davis started that way. If you plan to take this route, make sure that the person who is to hypnotize you is trained. Don't just go along with someone who "has read a couple of books on the subject"! There are certain inherent dangers in hypnotism; not so much in the state itself but in the reaction (or non-reaction) of the hypnotist to control situations. In other words, the hypnotist must be competent to handle anything that may arise.

Entering Trance (!)

For induction, many hypnotists will go through similar steps to the ones I gave you in Chapter Five, for meditation. They will go through the parts of your body, having you relax them and sink down deeper and deeper into relaxation and into hypnosis. The advantage of having a trained hypnotist take you down is that he can give certain tests, at various stages, to see how well you are responding and can determine just how deeply into trance you have progressed. He can monitor your progress every step of the way. Have the hypnotist give you instructions, while in trance, on how you can self-induce the state. In this way you can then later get away from relying on that second party.

One method of inducing trance yourself I give in *Amazing Secrets Of the Psychic World:*

> *Begin by gazing for some time at a bright object, such as reflected light coming from a mirror, crystal ball, etc. This will tend to tire the eyes and nerves slightly*

and bring about a dazed condition which is usually the beginning of trance. While looking at the bright object, breathe deeply and regularly through the nose and from the diaphragm. You must not let this distract your attention, however, as all the bodily processes should be unconscious. If you have already practiced deep breathing you should by this time be so far advanced that you can do so at will without consciously thinking of it.

While looking at the bright object do not concentrate or think of anything in particular beyond keeping yourself conscious and remembering all the time that you are "yourself," that you are not leaving your body, and that you are not going to become totally unconscious. During this process the room should be as quiet as possible, though some monotonous sound, such as the ticking of a large clock, might assist matters. Do not listen to this consciously, however; abolish all feelings of fear and all anxiety, as such mental states will effectually prevent you from entering the trance condition. "Let yourself go" and develop as far as possible.

When you feel you are in a good, relatively deep, trance state, give yourself a suggestion that will help bring about that same state on any future occasion. Give yourself a key word or phrase. For example, while in trance say to yourself, "Anytime in the future, when I want to go into trance for mediumistic purposes, I have only to relax, breathe deeply, and say to myself the word 'Spirit-state' and I will immediately be in a deep state of trance, even deeper than the one I am now in." (You can, of course, choose any word or make up one of your own. I

would suggest a word that you would not be likely to
use in everyday conversation . . . you don't want to
accidentally put yourself out when standing around
at a cocktail party!)

Early Symptoms

Many mediums will tell you that they passed through a
period when starting out when either they thought
themselves to be in great danger, or they thought they
were losing their minds! This, however, passes off as you
progress, and so they will assure you. You will certainly
find it easier, and much more reassuring, to be able to sit
with another experienced medium when you are first
developing. Unfortunately, of course, they are not easy
to find.

The oncoming of trance is sometimes signified by
certain physical and psychical manifestations which
should not alarm you when and if they appear. Cramps,
sudden pains — often abdominal — nausea, even hic-
coughs, these and others can be signs of developing
mediumship. You may see flashes of light, become suddenly faint, or feel that everything is rushing in upon
you. These are some of the symptoms you may experience when first you start sitting. And I do say *may* experience, for certainly not everyone goes through this. But if
you do, go with it. Keep sitting, knowing that these are
signs that trance and spirit contact are making themselves felt.

As a contrast to the unpleasant signs, you may go to
the other extreme and have the sensation of warmth and
beautiful flower scents and perfumes wafting about you.

You may have the sensation of falling slowly backwards and descending on a white cloud, hearing beautiful music and seeing wonderful sunrises and sunsets.

Rules For Development

There are three basic rules that professional mediums suggest. You should try to follow them.

1. Your mental and physical health must be good. If you feel depleted, exhausted, or run-down physically; if you are suffering from any disease or are full of fear, apprehension and doubts; or if anger rages, you may anticipate a difficult time in your development and unpleasant experiences throughout the slow process. Good diet and deep breathing exercises are wonderful aids to psychic development.

2. You should be careful to keep your conscious mind alert when first entering trance. Don't give up completely at the very beginning. Always keep in the background of your mind the thought: "I am myself; I am (name). I will remain in my body. I will not be influenced negatively. I will not be influenced against my will. I can always return to myself whenever I wish." It's not easy to keep thoughts going in your mind while, at the same time, becoming passive in all other ways, but do it.

3. Assure yourself, repeatedly, that you have a guide, a Guardian Angel, or however you wish to think of him or her. Reassure yourself that you have a whole band of spirits on the next level who are ready and anxious to help you.

Physical Conditions and Development Exercises

There are many books on spiritualism that say you must work in darkness, or near darkness. This is not so. Many very successful mediums not only work in the complete light of day, but insist on doing so. It is true that darkness seems to aid such physical phenomena as materializations, but for most work — clairvoyance, clairaudience, clairsentience, psychometry, automatism, etc. — there is no reason not to work in an open room in daylight or full artificial light. Make sure there is a good supply of fresh air in the room (No smokers!).

Soft, unobtrusive music seems to be a positive stimulant. "Unobtrusive" is the keyword; it can be classical, pop, or even rock, so long as it does not become obtrusive. Flowers in the room are also most welcome.

Personally I like to burn a little (very little) incense to add to the vibrations. Dried sage, in the Amerindian style, is good. But this latter would be very definitely a personal preference.

Make sure you have everything ready to hand before you go into trance. If you are going to need, or might need, pencils and paper (for automatic writing, perhaps), see that they are there.

A good practice in developing trance mediumship is to cultivate the habit of analyzing your "falling asleep" process. Try to catch yourself as you fall asleep and hold onto yourself in this semi-sleeping condition — what is known as the hypnagogic state — for as long as you can before actually dropping off to sleep. It won't be easy to do, but you will master it in time.

Remember that you are probably not going to develop into a great medium overnight! Spiritual progress is an individual thing, but many — if not most — mediums spent years in development. This doesn't mean you won't be able to "do anything" in all that time, it just means that it may take some time for you to be able to make spirit contact at all, to do so reliably and consistently, and to get used to mastering the difficulties of communication, interpretation, symbolism, etc., as I have spoken about them. But keep at it. You wouldn't expect to be able to pick up a violin and play it expertly if you had never handled one before. Look upon your spiritual gifts in a similar way to musical gifts; they will take time to develop and will need lots and lots of practice.

IX

Clairvoyance, Clairaudience, Clairsentience

"Clear Seeing"

"Clairvoyance" is derived from two French words: *clair* meaning "clear" and *voir* meaning "to see." In spiritualism, however, it means far more than that. It is used to cover, if not explain, a large number of different phenomena. It is, perhaps, the best known of psychic faculties.

Types of clairvoyance include the medium being able to see people and things on the Second Level; the spirit world. It also includes being able to see within the human body, and thereby diagnose disease (this is sometimes called "medical clairvoyance"). To see into closed areas, such as closets, boxes, safes, etc., is sometimes termed "x-ray clairvoyance." This would also cover the reading of sealed letters or billets (see Chapter Nineteen).

An extension of clairvoyance is the ability to see persons and objects in the future, which actually ties it in with *precognition* ("to know before"), or in the past — *retrocognition*. Psychometry and scrying (crystal-gazing) could also come under the general heading of clairvoyance.

Seeing the spirit world does not necessarily include being able to hear it, or hear those who appear. This is where the problems of interpretation arise, as I described in Chapter Six.

Many psychics and mediums say that the psychic centre for clairvoyance is situated at the position of the third eye — between and slightly above the two eyebrows. However, other mediums claim that the center is at the solar plexus, while still others say at the heart center. It is probably a personal matter . . . certain individuals work better through one particular center rather than another.

It is not always easy to tell the difference between true clairvoyant pictures and hallucinations. As with many other forms of psychic development, only later follow-up and verification can distinguish the truth from that which is apparent. For example, a medium might say, "I see an elderly couple. They appear to be in their eighties. The woman is short — about five feet two inches — the man tall and thin. Both are white-haired. Hers is pulled back in a bun, while his is brushed straight back and is showing signs of thinning on top. He wears glasses and has a drooping moustache . . ." The sitter might have absolutely no recollection of any such couple. To all intents and purposes it could well be that the medium was letting his or her imagination get away, was in touch with the wrong spirits, or was completely wrong for whatever reason. Yet later, on checking old family photo albums, the sitter may well find just such a couple, distantly related, revealed to him.

"Clear Hearing and Sensing"

Clairaudience, or "clear hearing," is similar to clairvoyance; it is the ability to hear sounds and voices on the other level. Many times a medium will seem to hear a voice whispering in her ear. To the medium this is quite distinct, as though someone is standing there beside her. Other times the words seem to come from inside the head. The classic example of this was, perhaps, Joan of Arc who, in the fifteenth century, followed the advice of her voices and led the French army against that of England. Joan had been hearing, and listening to, her voices since she was thirteen years old.

Clairsentience is neither actually seeing nor hearing but simply "sensing" in some way. "I get the feeling of such-and-such . . ." is the way the medium might put what she is picking up. The medium might feel hot or cold; might feel something of the pain experienced by the deceased; might sense the loneliness, the longing, the joy of the communicating spirit. All these could be sensed without ever actually seeing the spirit or hearing what they have to say.

Developing Clairvoyance

As I've said, clairvoyance is probably the most common and best known of psychic faculties. This is because we use our eyes more than any of our other organs of sense. The sight centers in the brain are used more than any others. In dreams, we "see" things more than we hear them. Our memory consists mainly of visual symbols — we pull up pictures of people and things when remembering, more than we do sounds, smells, etc.

Since these parts of the mind and brain are so active, it is only an extension of this faculty of inducing memory images which enables us to see figures and objects in clairvoyance.

Concentration is probably the most important part of clairvoyance. You must be able to concentrate on one particular object for several minutes without allowing anything else to enter your mind. As an exercise, take a simple object, such as an apple or a flower. Look at it and concentrate on it for five minutes. When you first do this you will find that after only a minute or so your mind will start to wander from the object. Don't let it. Really concentrate and review every part of the object. Then close your eyes and continue to see the object. As soon as it starts to fade, open your eyes to refresh your memory, then close them again.

From there pass on to photographs. Concentrate on someone's photograph. Let it be the photograph of just one person standing alone, preferably a head shot. Then be able to continue seeing the person with your eyes closed. Now, still with your eyes closed, see them slowly turn their head. Be able to see all the details of the head from these new angles.

If you have a friend who is willing to sit quietly (without talking) and let you concentrate on him or her, this is even better than a photograph. It also, of course, allows you to verify your "seeing" of the other angles of their head after you have mentally turned them.

From here proceed to actual events. Think of some particularly striking event that took place during the day. A small event — not too complex, with only two or three people involved. Recreate that event in your mind, with your eyes closed. See everything that happened. Really concentrate on it and pick up all the details. You will surprise yourself by noticing things that you didn't even realize you had noticed at the time.

Here is where you can make use of a modern tool — the VCR, or video recorder. Find, or make, a tape of some small but significant scene. (Any historical scene from a Public Television miniseries could be good.) Don't let it be too long; just a couple of minutes to start. Turn down the sound and watch the scene. Watch it several times over. Then close your eyes and recreate the scene in your mind. See if you can pick up all the small details. The great thing here is that you can go back and replay the tape as often as necessary to check on what you see.

Into Mediumship

Here are some more development exercises:

Sit comfortably in a chair that has good back support and, preferably, has arms on which to rest your own arms. If the chair is without arms, then let your hands rest loosely on your upper thighs, palms upwards. Feet flat on the floor, close your eyes and breathe deeply several times, doing your relaxation exercises and then your cleansing exercise of breathing in the white light and breathing out any negativity (see Chapter Five).

EXERCISE 1

Now picture a large tube, like a cardboard mailing tube, standing on its end on the floor in front of you. The ends of the tube are open. See yourself pick up the tube and look through it. "See" (with your eyes still closed) the wall of the room where you sit. Move the far end of the tube around and see the different objects in the room, the pictures on the wall, the furniture, etc. Open your eyes and verify.

Exercise 2

Now imagine that the tube is no longer simply a rigid cardboard one but is infinitely elastic; able to stretch away into the far distance. No matter how far it stretches, or how many turns and twists it makes, you are still able to see through it and clearly see what is at the far end.

Using the Visualization Tube

Mentally direct the end of the tube to the house of a friend or relative. See the outside of the house and notice all the detail. Then take the tube inside the house. Take it to various rooms and see them in all their detail. See if there is anyone in the house. Who is it? What are they doing? After this exercise, when you have returned to normalcy, as it were, telephone your friend or relative and find out if what you saw them doing was correct. You may be surprised to find that it was! However, if it was not, don't be discouraged. Keep practicing, going to various locations and seeing a number of different people and actions.

EXERCISE 3

The tube is now about a hundred yards long. At the end of it, see the face of a friend. See the face just as clearly as you possibly can. Adjust the tube like a telescope, to bring the face into full focus or to enlarge any particular detail(s). Now gradually shorten the length of the tube, drawing in the face towards you as the tube shortens. Bring it in till the tube is only inches long and the face is right there before you. Practice drawing in various people's faces, objects and scenes, so that you can see them at close range.

EXERCISE 4

Extend your tube and focus on the face of a deceased relative. Again draw that face in towards you and enlarge it; be able to examine it clearly from every angle. Readjust to a good comfortable length, as though the person were there in the room with you. Mentally ask how they are and listen for any response. Ask if they have any message for you, or for anyone else, and again listen carefully for a response.

You can see that Exercise 4 has led you into mediumship itself. In fact many mediums start exactly this way, with the mental tube, and for quite some time always work with it to bring themselves into contact with the second level. You don't really need the tube to make contact, of course, but it can be a very useful tool to get started.

You might want to insert another intermediate step between Exercise 3 and Exercise 4: Focus your tube on your guide or Doorkeeper. Bring him or her into focus and communicate. Then the guide can bring the spirits to the end of the tube (actually cutting out Exercise 4).

There is yet another variation you might like to try, especially if you have difficulty getting either your guide or a spirit to appear. Simply extend the tube and see, at the far end, the color green. Focus the tube and see that the green is actually green grass. Now open up the view — like a zoom lens on a camera opening to include a full scene — and see that it is a field with a person, or several people, standing on the grass. Now focus in on one or more of the people.

Alternatively, let the green that you see turn out to be the green fabric of an armchair. As you pull back, you are looking at the back of a chair and someone is sitting in it. Then, slowly, bring the end of the tube around the chair (or have the chair turn) so that you are able to see who is sitting in it.

There are many ways, such as these, to "sneak up on" the person you wish to see when you have difficulty simply zooming straight in on them.

Aids to Clairaudience

Most of us, as children, have held up a seashell to our ears and heard the "sounds of the sea." A similar practice can lead to the development of clairaudience.

Obtain a good size conch shell and hold it to your ear. You will again hear that distant roaring sound, as of the ocean. It is probably due to the air within the cavities of the shell and the resounding properties of the various inner curves of its surfaces. If you use two shells, and hold one to each ear, the experience will be doubled but may be extended even more than that.

Listening

If you sit quietly and do your lead-in exercise — head exercises plus deep breathing — then close your eyes and take up the shells, you can pick up sounds other than those I have just spoken of. Many psychics can hear distant voices. By concentrating you can frequently hear your own name being called. Once again you need to try to clear your mind as much as possible, thinking of nothing in particular. Just sit and listen. Starting with hearing their own name, many psychics then go on to distinguish other words and even to distinguish particular voices. Clairaudient messages can come through.

What you hear may be merely the externalizing of your own thoughts and auditory messages from the unconscious mind. But it may also be more than that, being telepathic or premonitory messages that are actual spirit communication. Much depends on the content of the message, of course. And, as with the above mentioned exercises, everything should be checked out so far as you are able. If you obtain a jumble of nonsense it is probably your own subconscious activity and may be disregarded. But if you obtain a characteristic and direct message, check it out to see if there is validity to it. As in so much of spiritual contact, you must use your own judgment as to the value of what you receive.

Shell hearing is an easy way of easing into clairaudience and can be very pleasant. The voices may emerge from a confused babble or from a mishmosh of sound, or they may come through loud and clear by themselves. You may immediately recognize the voices you pick up or you may not. If you do recognize them then, obviously, it will help prove their authenticity.

You may also pick up the sound of music from the shell. Sometimes this is significant insofar as it may be music especially associated with a particular spirit.

Psychic Telephone

A variation on the shells is to imagine a telephone. Start as with the clairvoyant tube, but instead of the tube imagine a telephone sitting on a small table in front of you. Know that when it rings there will be someone from the spirit world on the other end of the line. Then, hear it ring. Mentally pick up the receiver and put it to your ear. Again, you should hear someone call you by name and you may proceed from there. You can, of course, do this exercise with an actual (disconnected) telephone. Some people prefer this since, as with the shells, it gives them an actual physical object to hold. This can help strengthen an otherwise weaker imagination. Again as with the tube, you can get a "phone call" from your guide first, who will then bring others to the phone to talk to you.

One word of warning: if, after stopping listening to the shell(s) or telephone, you continue to hear voices, immediately stop all such experiments, at least for several days. You are probably just straining too hard to capture something. Don't — either in this or the above clairvoyant experiments — try too hard. Concentrate, yes, but *don't strain*. The phenomena should happen fairly easily, gradually easing into your awareness. Spiritual contact should not be a strain nor in any way distressful.

Scrying, or Crystal-gazing

Crystal-gazing, otherwise known as scrying, is another way of getting into clairvoyance. However, a possible problem is coming to rely on the crystal and not being able to make contact without it. This is because you are externalizing the visions rather than producing/receiving them inside your own head.

The crystal or glass ball you use should be of about three to four inches in diameter and as clear as possible (i.e., free of bubbles or other defects). If you cannot obtain a ball you can do this exercise using a tumbler of water, filled to the brim. Let this be a clear, unpatterned glass. Ball or glass, stand it on a piece of black cloth (velvet is best) so that when you look down into it there is nothing immediately around that will distract your attention.

As with all the above exercises, sit in a quiet room where you will not be disturbed, and do your preliminary breathing and relaxation. Have the crystal ball on a table in front of you, at a comfortable height. If you prefer you may hold it in the palm of your hand, though I recommend using the table at least to start with. With this form of clairvoyance it is a good idea to start by working in a semi-darkened room, any light being behind you as you sit.

Close your eyes and try to make your mind blank. Then open them, and gaze into the crystal. Still try to keep the mind blank (not easy!). Try to look into the center of the ball rather than the surface. One of two things will eventually happen. You may immediately see someone or something in the ball or you may see the ball seemingly start to fill with white smoke. If it is the latter, the smoke will fill the ball then will gradually dissipate and leave a scene of a person or thing. The smoke filling the ball is known as "clouding." If in your case the smoke should be grey, or even black, don't panic — the color is not significant!

Don't be concerned if you get nothing at all the first time you try this. Keep looking for about ten minutes. Much longer than that and you will merely be straining your eyes. Give up and try again the next day. Some people see images right away but many more have to try for days (or even weeks) before getting results. The secret — if secret there is — is as with so much in psychic development: do not strain to get results. Just relax and let it happen. Don't try to keep the eyes unblinking; just blink naturally when necessary.

The scene that you see will be like looking at a miniature television screen. It will usually be in color (though some few people do only see in black and white), and may be a still picture but is more likely to be moving. What you see can be anything. To start with you probably won't have much control over what comes. But as you progress, start out by meditating on what you want to see, then do your mind-clearing and go into the gazing. Then you will probably see what or whom you had mentally asked for. As in the above exercises, it's a good plan to try to contact your guide first.

Scrying

X

~o~o~o~o~o~o~o~o~o~o~o~o~o~o~o~o~o~o~o~o~

PSYCHOMETRY

Touching the Past

From the Greek words *psyche* ("soul") and *metron* ("measure") we get the word "psychometry." To psychometrize an object is to hold it and sense from its vibrations a part, or the whole, of the object's history. To help explain it, Hereward Carrington related the story of a Professor Denton, a minerologist. Denton's wife was a gifted psychometrist. When he gave her a specimen to hold from a carboniferous formation, she closed her eyes and immediately started describing swamps, trees with tufted heads and scaled trunks, and great frog-like creatures that lived in that age. He then gave her lava from a Hawaiian volcanic eruption. She held it and described a "boiling ocean;" a cataract of golden lava. Denton's mother, who did not believe in psychometry, was given a meteorite to hold. She said: "I seem to be traveling away, away through nothing — I see what looks like stars and mist." Denton's wife gave a similar description, adding that she saw a revolving tail of sparks.

Another good example is of a psychometrist who, as a test, was handed a sealed package. After holding it for a moment the psychometrist said that he felt he was in a very small room which either had no windows or whose windows seemed painted over with white paint. He felt extreme anxiety. He went on to say that the package he was holding contained a green book which could explain his feelings. When it was opened, the package was found to contain a green-bound book which was the logbook from a small boat that used to travel regularly between England and Ireland. The last entry in the log was written by the Captain as he strained to see out through the windows of the enclosed bridge and through a thick fog which enveloped the ship. Needless to say, the captain was feeling very worried, situated as he was in a busy shipping lane.

Psychometry is something which most people possess and can be brought out with just a little practice. Experiments have shown that it is especially strong in one out of every ten men who try it, and in one out of every four women. It can be a useful tool for the medium. To be able to pick up a bracelet, a ring, a brooch or a watch, for example, that once belonged to someone is to be able to tune in on that person almost immediately. It can be a way to make the necessary contact with the spirit for communication.

Psychic Aura Exercises

Every object gives off certain emanations, or vibrations. With practice you can develop the sense to pick up on these vibrations. Gather together a selection of objects such as small pieces of wood, metal and stone, bits of cloth fabric and leather. Choose some that are of similar size and texture, such as pieces of cloth, fur and leather or bits of wood, stone and metal.

Sitting quietly, take each of the objects in your hands, one at a time, and concentrate on it. Feel its texture. Think of its origins. See the tree from which the wood came; see the animal whose fur you handle, and so on. Spend as long as feels comfortable with each piece. You'll probably be able to concentrate best by closing your eyes as you work. Do this as an exercise at least once a day for several days. You will gradually come to receive your impressions almost as soon as you touch the object.

Then start keeping your eyes closed so that you don't really know which object you are picking up. Sure, you'll be able to feel the difference between, say, a piece of metal and a piece of felt, but what about between bamboo and oak, or tin and copper? To further keep your physical senses out of it, place each sample in an envelope. Pick up the envelope on the palm of one hand and gently close the palm of the other over it. In this way you shouldn't be able to "guess" what you are holding but have to depend more on your psychic impressions.

Keep a record of your exercises in a notebook. Number the envelopes and make up a list of the different objects, together with the number or letter assigned to each, in a column down the left side of the first page:

Actual Content	Envelope Number
Cotton	A
Silk	B
Velvet	C
Snakeskin	D
Seashell	E
Wool	F
Ivory	G
Clay	H
Iron	I
Bamboo	J
Oak	K
Feather	L

Draw a number of columns, vertically, across the page, headed "Impressions" and numbered 1, 2, 3, etc.

Lay the envelopes, numbered side down, on the table and pick them up one at a time and try to blend with the contents, to find what it is. You might "see" the object itself or you might simply pick up its background — you might see the small piece of wood or you might see a single tree or a whole forest of oak trees. On another piece of paper, write down your impression — "#1: Oak." Place the envelope to one side and pick up another. Work at that, record your impression, and place the envelope to the right of the first. Work through them all, being careful to lay them down in the order in which you worked with them.

When you have finished, look at your results. Let's say that your first impression was of oak. Turn over the first envelope and see what its number is. Perhaps it is E — seashell. In your column of "Impressions" under "1," write "Oak" alongside seashell. Recording all your guesses will give you something that looks like this:

Actual Content	Envelope Number	Impressions 1	2	3	4	5
Cotton	A	Silk				
Silk	B	Cotton				
Velvet	C	Wool				
Snakeskin	D	Ivory				
Seashell	E	Oak				
Wool	F	Shell				
Ivory	G	Feather				
Clay	H	Iron				
Iron	I	Velvet				
Bamboo	J	Oak				
Oak	K	Oak				
Feather	L	Clay				

You can see that although you only got one right (Oak) you got several very close (A, B, C, J). Repeat the exercise a number of times. After a while you will find that your impressions are getting better; you are at least picking up the woods as woods and the cloth as cloth, with several "right on the money."

Actual Content	Envelope Number	Impressions 1	2	3	4	5
Cotton	A	Silk	Cotton	Silk	Wool	Cotton
Silk	B	Cotton	Silk	Velvet	Silk	Silk
Velvet	C	Wool	Feather	Bamboo	Velvet	Wool
Snakeskin	D	Ivory	Feather	Snakeskin	Oak	Feather
Seashell	E	Oak	Ivory	Shell	Ivory	Shell
Wool	F	Shell	Oak	Velvet	Wool	Wool
Ivory	G	Feather	Shell	Ivory	Ivory	Ivory
Clay	H	Iron	Iron	Clay	Velvet	Feather
Iron	I	Velvet	Snakeskin	Ivory	Iron	Silk
Bamboo	J	Oak	Velvet	Bamboo	Oak	Bamboo
Oak	K	Oak	Wool	Oak	Oak	Oak
Feather	L	Clay	Wool	Cotton	Velvet	Snakeskin

You can see that there is a very definite pattern emerging. The more you practice, the higher rate of accuracy you will achieve. With several absolutely right, there are also several that are very close, with certain similar types often confused. Keep on, practicing over a number of days or even weeks. You will find that you will eventually be able to score correctly most of the time.

From there take the next step. Place various photographs of people in different envelopes (each photograph being of just one person). You will find, in fact, that this is easier than working with the objects. You will find that you pick up not only the physical appearance of the person whose photograph you are working with, but also a variety of facts about them — their likes and dislikes, residence, habits, employment, hobbies, etc. Keep records and see how you progress.

From there, borrow small objects from friends. If they are all similar objects, such as all rings, you probably won't need to place them in envelopes (though don't confuse whose is whose when you go to return them!). Ask yourself questions other than "To whom does this belong?" For example, ask yourself "How long has this person had this item?" "Where did it come from?" "How old is it?" See if you can get the history of the piece and then, also, more details of the person who owns it. It should be needless to say that you will need to verify what you get with the owner.

The final step is to borrow objects which have belonged to the deceased relatives or friends of your acquaintances. Here you certainly will not need to place the object in an envelope. You can simply hold it in your hand while the friend is present . . . as you will do when working as a medium.

Spirit Speaks First

Relay everything you pick up from the object, both about its previous owner and all that you can get connected with that person. Again, get as much verified as possible. I cannot stress too strongly that you must not be afraid to say what you feel. No matter how "silly" or "stupid" it seems, logically, to state something about an object you are holding, go ahead and say it. It has been said that the spirit speaks first and you speak second. In other words, the first impression you get is invariably the correct one, coming from spirit. The second impression is coming

Practicing Psychometry

more from your conscious or unconscious reasoning and may not be correct at all. So, no matter how it sounds, speak up with the very first impressions you get.

Analyze your sensations and emotions as best you can, after that first impression has been received. See what you feel or experience within yourself. Then express this in words, to the best of your ability. These emotions often express, in that form, facts which could not be expressed in any other way, though they apparently have no connection whatsoever with the object you are holding. For example, if you are holding a bracelet and you get, in connection with it, a feeling of deep depression followed by sudden difficulty breathing and sensations of water, of suffocating and drowning, say all of this. State it as fully as you are able. It may be that the person who owned the bracelet drowned herself in a fit of melancholy! In this way the emotions you recognize are fully in accordance with the sensations which you receive from the object.

Side Benefits

You will find that there is a side benefit to developing your psychometry. You will find that when you meet people for the first time, simply by shaking hands you will pick up on them and on their feelings and emotions. Rather like "Counselor Troi" of the popular television series *Star Trek: The Next Generation,* you will become something of an empath. Though, unlike Troi, you will need to make physical contact with the person to pick up on him or her.

Different Readings for Different Mediums

Don't be surprised if you and another medium both read from the same object and get different stories. An object that has been around for a while may pass through many hands. What one medium tunes into may be from a totally different period from that tuned into by another medium. Even from an object that has had only one owner, what you tune into may be from one aspect, or one period, of the owner's life while the other medium may pick up on a quite different phase or interest of that same owner.

It may be claimed that the deceased had owned a particular object for many, many years. Yet — perhaps unbeknownst to the living relative — the object may well have belonged to someone else at some point; perhaps someone with particularly strong emanations that really pervade the object. To give a physical parallel, it is a little like a chair that started out painted in a dark color but was subsequently painted over with white paint. Outwardly the chair is, then, white and everyone may remember it as only being white. Yet to someone with a sensitive eye, the dark paint still shows through.

Psychometry as a Tool in Spirit Communication

What is the place of psychometry in spirit communication? From what I have said it would seem that there is no necessary connection between the object being read and the spirit of that owner now "existing" on the Second Level. We can learn about the deceased as they were, when alive and owning the object, but that doesn't necessarily help make a connection with their spirit.

In practice, though, it seems it does help make the connection. Especially if the object is one that was dear to the deceased. By virtue of holding that object and concentrating upon it to align with its vibrations, you frequently do also tune to the wavelength, as it were, of the owner. He or she may not be making a point of staying close to the object, yet there is some sort of an emotional thread, or wavelength, that is still intact. Simply by practicing psychometry on an object we can often tune in more easily to the deceased.

XI

TABLE TIPPING AND LEVITATION

Choice of Table

Table tipping is another method of spirit communication that was very popular in the early days of spiritualism. It has fallen a little out of favor in modern times mainly because it came to be treated as little more than a parlor game by many. Table tipping is simplicity itself. If anything, it is too easy. Consequently many people tried it and, finding that it came easily, misused it. Like all psychic phenomena, and spirit communication in particular, you need to approach it with a certain amount of respect. There is room for humor, yes, but not ridicule.

Serious table tippers can cause large, heavy tables to move. Tables which could not easily be moved under normal circumstances by the total number of persons present can almost dance around the room under psychic influences.

But to start, choose a small, light table. A card table is ideal. Or you can make your own. Lumber stores sell table tops (rectangular or circular) and table legs. Use wooden ones rather than metal or plastic. A round top about thirty inches in diameter can work well, though the actual size will depend upon how many people are to

119

regularly use it. Attach three or four legs equidistant around it. The legs should be of a comfortable height; again thirty inches is good. If you are planning on working with a regular circle of friends (see Chapter Seventeen), and need to take your table to different homes, it can be useful to have a table where the legs can be unscrewed for traveling. With four legs I would suggest they be perpendicular to the table top, but with a three-legged table, set them in from the edge and have them sloping out (you can buy the necessary fittings either flat or angled).

Circle of Hands

You don't need to sit in a darkened room for table tipping. Many people do prefer the light to be slightly dimmed, but even that is not mandatory. You can work in full daylight. But try different degrees of light to see which works best for you.

However many persons are participating should sit evenly spaced around the table. Start this, as any psychic exercise, as I described in Chapter Five. Everyone should have their feet flat on the floor, hands loosely in their laps (you will put your hands on the table after this preliminary exercise). Breathe deeply and calm yourself. Then, as you breathe, imagine you are breathing in the soft, positive, blue light of protection. Feel it filling your body and driving out any negativity. As you continue to breathe it in, see it expanding to fill the circle of friends about the table. Continue to breathe deeply until the light expands to fill the whole room in which you all sit.

If you feel so inclined you may all say a prayer. Many spiritualists sing a song together to help create a pleasant, happy atmosphere. It should certainly be a light, happy song. It does not have to be a hymn or anything religious . . . so many Christian hymns are heavy and depressing, anyway! The purpose of the singing is simply to help attune the sitters to one another and to create a pleasant atmosphere into which you may invite the spirit.

Now all should lay their hands on the table, palms down, along the edge. Initially it is a good idea to make an unbroken circle of the hands. Touch your two thumbs together, spread your fingers and have your little fingers touching the little fingers of the people on either side.

As the medium, you will be the spokesperson. It can get very confusing if everyone just tries to shout out questions. Let the others relay their questions through you. Better yet, start with a list of predetermined questions (though, as you progress, you will need to be more spontaneous, interacting with the spirit you contact).

Start by asking aloud, "Is there anybody there?" Repeat this a few times. You can add: "If there's anybody there, would you please communicate by moving the table?" You should shortly feel the table start to move. Perhaps it will give a creak or two to start, or it may immediately start to rock back and forth. Don't be alarmed; after all, this is what you've been waiting for! Continue to say, "Please communicate by moving the table."

Thumps of Intelligence

The table will start to rock up onto two legs and thump back down onto the floor. When it has done this a few times say: "Please tip twice for yes and three times for no. Are you of the spirit world?" The table will respond by thumping twice.

Why two thumps for yes and three for no? These are used, rather than simply one for yes and two for no, so that there is no doubt about a response. Sometimes there is only a slight response and you are not quite certain whether it really was a thump or not. If you have asked for two as a minimum, then there is never any doubt that you are getting a reply.

Once contact has been established you may proceed with questions. Initially stick to those questions that can be answered yes or no. You will get information faster that way and it will give everyone time to get used to the feelings of communicating.

The actual force which initially moves the table is the force of the combined muscle power of the sitters. By that I don't mean that the sitters are consciously making the table rock. It is the spirit who makes use of that muscle power to do the physical moving but then directs it to provide the intelligence; to provide the answers to the questions asked. You move it, yes, but the spirit provides the answers that come through it. (You'll find that it's possible for things to be moved *without* the direct help of sitters, but at this stage don't worry about it.)

Question and Answer

When you have got the hang of getting yes/no answers go on to having actual messages spelled out. Say: "To elaborate on answers, please bang the table once for the letter A, twice for B, three times for C, and so on." You can then ask if there are any messages for anyone in particular (rather than spelling out complete names, go by initials). Thumping down on the floor so many times for the letters of the alphabet can seem long and tedious at first but it is surprising how quickly it can go. Many times, also, you can cut down by guessing what is being spelled, half way through the word, and saying something like: "Do you mean 'summertime' (or whatever the word)?"

The information obtained from the table may surprise you. Keep a careful record of all questions asked and all answers received. Appoint someone not sitting at the table as Secretary, to keep the record. Check out as much information as you are able. You will be surprised at how much is relevant. There will, however, be some which is pure nonsense or even gibberish. It seems that many spirits are desperate to make contact with the physical world . . . with anyone on this plane. They will joyfully come through the table and talk for the pure joy of being in contact. If you are looking for contact with a particular individual — perhaps a dead relative — they may not be averse to pretending to be that relative, just so that they can stay in contact. So don't take anything at its face value. Check and re-check.

When you have already established contact with your guide, as we discussed in Chapter Seven, you can usually get him or her to take charge of "the other side" of the table. Then you have someone to keep the pretenders and foolers at bay! You can ask for specific spirits to come to you through the table, and if they are available you will be put in contact.

Levitation

The table will sometimes go up on just one leg. There have been many séances in which I have participated, where the table has gone up on one leg and spun around rapidly. People had to leave their seats and rush around, trying to keep their hands on the table surface!

The next step from there would seem to be for all the legs of the table to come off the ground, levitating the table. Although this is a most uncommon occurrence, it has happened many times throughout the history of spiritualism. It seems totally unbelievable, perhaps, and yet photographs have been taken validifying the levitations. Some of these photographs have been taken with infrared film, where the phenomenon has taken place in a darkened séance room.

Levitation, and table-tipping itself, comes under the heading of "physical" phenomena. In *Mysterious Psychic Forces* (London 1907), Camille Flammarion includes some very clear photographs of a table fully levitated at a séance with the famous medium Eusapia Paladino. This took place during an investigation of the medium by various leading men of the time, including Professors Lombroso, Richet, Buffern, Gerosa and Schiaparelli. Flammarion described it as follows:

> *This levitation, one of the most frequent phenomena that occur in the experiments with Eusapia, stood a most satisfactory examination.*
>
> *The phenomenon always materialized under the following conditions: the persons seated about the table place their hands on it, and form the chain; each hand of the medium is held by the adjacent hand of her two neighbors; each of her feet remains under the feet of her neighbor, who also press her knees with theirs. She is seated, as usual, at one of the small ends of the (rectangular) table, a position least favorable for a mechanical levitation. At the end of several minutes the table makes a slight movement, rises first to the right then to the left, and finally mounts off of its four feet straight into the air, and*

lies there horizontally (as if it were floating on a liquid), ordinarily at a height of from 4 to 8 inches (in exceptional cases from 24 to 27 inches); then falls back and rests on its four feet. It frequently remains in the air for several seconds, and while there also makes undulatory motions, during which the position of the feet under the table can be thoroughly examined. During the levitation the right hand of the medium often leaves the table, as well as that of her neighbor, and is held in the air above.

In order to better observe this thing, we removed one by one the persons placed at the table, recognizing the truth that the chain formed by several persons was neither necessary for this phenomenon nor for others. Finally, we left only a single person with the medium, seated at her left. This person placed her foot upon Eusapia's two feet and one hand upon her knees, and held with her other hand the left hand of the medium. Eusapia's right hand was on the table, in full view — though sometimes she held it in the air during the levitation.

As the table remained in the air for several seconds, it was possible to obtain several photographs of the performance. Three pieces of photographic apparatus were working together in different parts of the room . . . twenty photographs were obtained, some of which were excellent.

This gives some idea of the care that was taken to ensure there was no trickery or fraud, conscious or unconscious. One interesting point is that the fact of the circle being broken — people dropping out and moving away from the table — had no effect on the medium or her phenomenon. Usually mediums are insistent that the chain not be broken. Nandor Fodor (*Encyclopedia of Psychic Science*, London 1934) tells of an occurrence, in London in the late 1800s, in the house of Mrs. Guppy-Volckman when the American medium Mary Hardy was visiting.

Levitation of Mediums

Apparently Mrs. Volckman didn't wish to take part in that evening's séance and so she retired to the far end of the long room. Mrs. Hardy prepared herself with a circle of participants up the other end. As Fodor says:

> *Suddenly Mrs. Volckman was levitated and carried in sight of us all into the middle of the ring. As she felt herself rising in the air she called out: "Don't let go hands, for Heaven's sake!" We were just standing in a ring and I had hold of the hand of Prince Albert of Solme. As Mrs. Volckman came sailing over our heads, her feet caught his neck and mine, and in our anxiety to do as she told us we gripped tight hold of each other and were thrown forward on our knees by the force with which she was carried past us into the centre of the ring. The influence that levitated her, moreover, placed her on a chair with such a bump that it broke the two front legs off.*

Levitation of the table-tipping table is one thing; levitation of an actual person is quite another. Yet, again, there are several instances of just that, the above being but one example. Another example is the various levitations of Daniel Dunglas Home, which are legendary (see Chapter Four) and by far the best known.

Colin Evans Levitating
(Photo Courtesy of Psychic Press, Ltd.)

Amedee Zuccarini of Bologne frequently levitated. He was the subject of intense investigation by Dr. L. Patrizi, Professor of Physiology at the University of Modena, and Professor Creste Murani of the Milan Polytechnic. Many flashlight photographs were taken which showed Zuccarini suspended in midair with no visible signs of support. In 1938 excellent photographs were also taken of British medium Colin Evans levitating about three feet off the ground in London's Conway Hall during a public séance.

Under or Over?

A question often asked is, does the power which lifts the table come from underneath the table or from above it? It might be assumed that it comes from underneath, giving added credulity to charges that the medium somehow lifts the table with his or her foot, or otherwise. But Colin Brookes-Smith developed and set up electronic apparatus to determine the source of the "lift." So far his research indicates that in fact the lift comes from above the table!

Flammarion's earlier experiments with Eusapia Paladino included measurement of pressure on the table. Eusapia was made to sit alone at the table, in full light. She had her sleeves rolled up to the elbows and stuck her legs straight out in front of her (under the table) but repeatedly struck her feet together loudly, so that it was obvious she could not be using her legs in any way on the table. The investigators were constantly about her, observing everything.

The table itself was lifted along one side to a height of about six inches and suspended to a dynamometer which was coupled to a cord, in turn tied to a small beam supported across two wardrobes. With the medium's hands on either side of the dynamometer connection, on top of the table, the meter read 77 pounds. One would normally expect the reading to increase, with everyone's hands on the top surface, if pressure was applied. Instead the reading fell off until it reached only seven pounds, then four, then two, and finally zero! When conditions were reversed, with all hands under the table and Eusapia even turning her hands, so that the backs only were in contact, again instead of the expected decrease, the meter showed an increase to seven and a half and then on up to thirteen pounds!

Many such experiments have been done over the years. About the only conclusion that has been reached is that the medium is in no way responsible for the movement of the table; its lifting or dropping. If anything, the table seems to move directly contrary to the forces that may be applied.

Whether or not you get your table to completely levitate is not important. The main thing is to be able to use it to communicate with the spirits of the dead. Through table tipping you can talk with your loved ones and they with you. Keep a record of all that you do and carefully check out all the information you receive. Only in this way will you be able to verify, to your own satisfaction, whether or not you are truly in touch with Level Two.

XII

TALKING BOARDS

Ancient Form of Communication

Many people experience their first brush with "the occult" through the talking board. This is an ancient form of communicating with spirits of the dead, being known in China and in Greece from as early as 600 BC. Today there are several commercially produced boards on the market, one of the originals being the "Ouija" board (from the French *oui* and the German *ja,* both meaning "yes") of William Fuld, first commercially produced in 1892 and now marketed by Parker Brothers. This is a smooth-surfaced, rectangular board with the letters of the alphabet written across it in two curving lines. Below the letters are the numbers one through nine, zero, and the words "Yes," "No," and "Goodbye." With the board comes a sliding pointer, or *planchette,* which rests on three felt-covered feet and has a circular, clear plastic window through which the letters of the board can be read as it slides around.

The *modus operandi* for the board is for two people to sit facing one another with the board resting between them, on their knees. At the outset the planchette sits in the center of the board and the participants each have their fingers resting lightly on it. By gliding about the board and stopping over different letters, the planchette spells out messages and answers to questions put to it. It moves seemingly of its own volition, not from either person pushing it.

Let's look at a typical case of someone who has never used a talking board before.

Jim Waite had been invited to his first séance. He was sitting opposite his hostess, Mary Wilson. After a few moments, in response to Mary's repeated "Is there any spirit present?" the planchette started sliding across the board to the word "Yes." It was quite a firm movement and Jim had no doubt that it was Mary Wilson who was causing it: he was sure she was pushing it.

"Do you have any message for any person here?" asked Mary of the board.

"Yes," repeated the planchette. It then proceeded to slide around to point directly at "J," "I" and "M" . . . Jim! However, Jim himself remained unimpressed. So he remained until the planchette, continuing on its way, spelled out a message: "LOOK ONE MORE TIME BUTCH." Suddenly he became very much interested. "Butch" was the nickname of a favorite uncle who had recently died. Mary knew nothing of either the uncle or his nickname. Not only that but the message itself made a lot of sense. After Uncle Butch had died Jim had spent many hours going through his uncle's effects looking for a particular book that had been promised him. Jim had been unable to find it and had virtually given up the search. Now here was a message that fit that situation and something of which Mary Wilson could have no knowledge.

Can we now, then, assume that the message came from Jim's dead Uncle Butch? No . . . or, at least, not yet. The message obviously clears Mary of pushing the planchette, but it doesn't clear Jim himself. Obviously he was not consciously pushing it, but he might have been doing so *unconsciously*. At the back of his mind was the frustration of the search for the book. He might even have had some vague thought of Uncle Butch coming through at the séance to tell him where the book was. So long as the information received is known to at least one person present, then you can never rule out extra sensory perception rather than spiritual contact. What would have clinched it, in this case, would have been if the board had gone on to tell Jim exactly where the book was hidden. (It didn't do that, though it did inspire him to look one more time and, as it happens, Jim did find the book in that final search.)

As with automatic writing, it is the muscle power of the participants that actually causes the movement of the planchette. The question is, what is the source of the intelligence directing that use of the muscle power? The short answer seems to be, in many cases, spirits of the dead. A great deal of interesting research can be done with a talking board. Additionally a lot of fun may be had.

Commercial Faults

With the commercially produced boards there are, in my opinion, two faults. One is but a slight inconvenience, and that is when the planchette goes to the extremities of the board, one foot of the planchette may slip over the edge. You then must lift it back onto the board before you can continue. This is merely an aggravation, though it does interfere with the smooth run from letter to letter.

The second fault is more serious. It is in the design of the planchette. The instructions given (with the Ouija board) say: "The mysterious message indicator (planchette) will commence to move . . . as it passes over Ouija talking board each letter of a message is received as it appears through the transparent window covered by the message indicator." This is not strictly true. Sometimes you receive a string of letters that seem to make no sense whatsoever — until it is realized that the planchette is no longer showing the relevant letters through its plastic "window" on the one line, but is pointing to the letters on the line above with its tapered end! Consequently you must often watch, and note, two sets of letters rather than one! To overcome this drawback, I suggest covering over the "window" and going solely by where the pointed end of the planchette indicates. Some other talking boards (and the original Fuld design) do not have the "window" — they are just a solid, heart-shaped pointer — and so it is a simple matter to see what letters are indicated.

The indication in the instructions that only two people may operate the board at any one time is also incorrect. The board should be placed in the center of a small table and a number of people (four, five or even six) can then sit around and each place a fingertip on the edge of the planchette. In this way you will give far more energy to the board and receive back much more energetic responses.

Do It Yourself Talking Board

An older way of using the board is not to have an actual board at all. Simply print the letters of the alphabet on pieces of paper or card and lay them in a circle around the edge of a table. Include in the circle the words "Yes" and "No." "Goodbye" and "Rephrase" are also two useful things to include. Now upturn a wineglass in the center and use that as your planchette, resting fingertips on the rim of its upturned base. You will find that the wineglass will glide around the tabletop and stop at letters working just as well, if not better, than a commercial board.

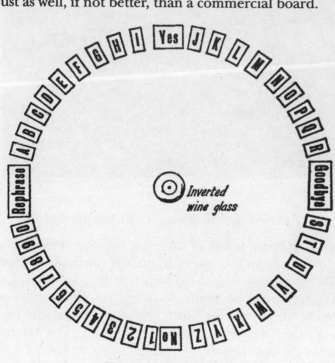

Homemade Talking Board

"Goodbye" is nice to have included, since it is only polite to bid farewell to the spirits at the conclusion of the evening, and they also like to be able to say goodbye to you. "Rephrase" can be useful. Sometimes you will ask a question and get no response. It might be that the question you have asked is ambiguous and you haven't realized it. If the wineglass goes to "Rephrase" then you can do just that; put the question another way.

Using a Talking Board

Record Keeping and a Spokesperson

Record keeping is one of the most important aspects of all forms of psychic research, and of spiritualism especially. Appoint a Secretary; someone to take notes. Let that person not be in on touching the planchette but concentrate on writing down everything asked and noting all the letters indicated in responses. The human memory is notoriously unreliable, so write down everything. An additional safeguard might be to have a tape recorder running also. (Certainly use a tape if there are only two of you present.)

One person, and one person only, should act as Spokesperson. If anyone else has a question, let them give it to the Spokesperson to ask. Different people asking different questions, sometimes more than one trying to speak at the same time, can be very confusing, even in everyday life! You can certainly make a change to a different Spokesperson after a time, but the changeover should be definite and announced to the spirits. In fact it is a good idea to try different people in the position, for some seem to have more success, and draw better response, than do others. But don't make the changeovers too frequently; give each person a reasonable amount of time in the position.

It's a good idea to prepare a list of questions before the sitting. This way there will be no long pause while everyone racks their brains to think of what to ask. This also helps the Secretary if all he or she has to do is fill in the answers and not have to also write out long questions as they are thought of and asked.

Procedure and Verification

There is no need to work in subdued light. Start your séance in the same way I described in the last chapter. Create a harmonious atmosphere, establish a protective barrier, and simply relax and enjoy it.

The Spokesperson starts by asking, in a normal voice, "Is there anybody there?" The question is repeated until the glass, or planchette, starts to glide across to the answer "Yes." It should then return to the center. If it doesn't return, simply ask it to: "Thank you. Will you please return to the center?"

For this initial movement it may be that you will have to sit and wait, asking if anyone is there, for five or ten minutes. This is especially so when you haven't used a board before. How quickly you get a response, and the "power" of that response, will depend on many factors including the attunement of the sitters, their acceptance, the willingness of the spirits to communicate, and their ability to do so.

At no time should anyone present attempt to push the planchette. This is most important. It should not be necessary to say but it seems that often there is someone present who is tempted. Certainly it is easy to do, without anyone knowing. You can get a few laughs at the expense of your friends . . . but what is the point? It would be so easy to do that it is certainly not "clever." You can, and should, approach the whole talking board experience with a sense of enjoyment; of pleasure. But at the same time it should be a serious approach (something of a dichotomy, perhaps) in that you don't want to be wasting your time there and you do want to receive appropriate material.

When you first start using a board you are bound to think, at some point, that someone *is* pushing it, as shown in the example I gave, above, of Jim Waite and Mary Wilson. It is a natural suspicion, but try to get it behind you and you will soon find it allayed.

After establishing contact, the sitting may proceed on lines such as the following:

"Is there anybody there, please?"

YES

"Are you willing to speak with us?"

YES

"Do you have a message for anyone here?"

YES

"Would you please give the name or initials of that person?"

J B D

"Is the message for John?"

YES

"Please spell out the message."

WAIT FOR THE SMUMRF

"Would you please repeat the last word?"

SUMMER

"Thank you. Carry on with the message."
NOW IS TOSOON
"Do you mean, 'Now is too soon'?"
YES
"Is there more to the message?"
NO

This is typical of the way the communication can go. Once in a while the letters may get a little jumbled and you will need to break in to straighten them out. Don't hesitate to ask questions if the incoming message is not clear. If there is any doubt about anything simply ask for a repeat. In the above example where "Wait for the smumrf" appears, not only are the letters of the last word jumbled but there is an "F" given instead of an "E." It could have been that the pointer moved too close to one letter rather than to the one next to it, or it might have stopped between the two. If that happens, and the Secretary is unsure which is meant, the Spokesperson should be asked to clarify it.

It can also happen that the spirit mistakes a letter. We don't know just how clearly it is possible to see from one level to another but it is easy to mistake between the letters H, K, and N, for example; or C, G, O and Q; or D, P, R and B . . . just try reading an eye-chart!

When a long message is being spelled out it can sometimes help your understanding of it by having the pointer pause briefly, in the center, to indicate the end of a sentence. In fact I have used the technique of asking the spirit to move the planchette all around the circle once at the end of a word and three times at the end of each sentence, to be quite sure. There have been times when the spirit has seemed impatient to get on with the message and the glass has absolutely raced around that circle!

As with so much of psychical research it is the follow-up, the verification after the séance, that can be most interesting. Did the spirit really live at the time claimed and is its body/shell buried where it stated? Can a grave be found? Check burial records, church records, public records, newspaper reports and obituaries; anything that might help. Was the spirit ever in the army or navy? Check military records.

Cross Correspondence

If you have sufficient number of people interested in talking boards to form two groups — this can be done with a minimum of four people; two sets of two — you can experiment in what is known as "cross correspondence." Let's call our two groups "A" and "B." Let's also appoint an unbiased Coordinator.

Start with each group advising its particular spirit contact of what they wish to do. This can be done in this fashion:

Spokesperson: "We want to do a cross-correspondence with our other group. They are meeting at Michelle's house, 115 Main Street, tomorrow night at 9:00 PM. During our sitting here tonight, please start a message that you will continue with them."

Then somewhere within the material that each group receives will be part of a message. On the face of it there will be nothing unusual. It may blend in with whatever else is received. But each group will send the record of its sitting to the Coordinator. He or she should be an intelligent, fairly learned person. The Coordinator's job is to search through both sets of material and find a total message. Let me give you an example to clarify this.

Let's suppose that among the many pages of Group A's material the Coordinator finds this:

"What sort of place are you in now?"

IT IS VERY PLEASANT, AS THOUGH THE WINTER IS PAST, THE RAIN IS OVER AND GONE AND EVERYTHING IS NICE AND FRESH AGAIN. ALMOST A REBIRTH.

Something suddenly strikes the Coordinator as sounding vaguely familiar. Very carefully going through Group B's equally lengthy material turns up:

"Was there anything you knew on this level that you miss?"

NO

"Can everything be experienced where you are, then?"

YES

"The different seasons?"

OH, YES. EVEN WHEN THE FLOWERS APPEAR ON THE EARTH, THE TIME OF THE SINGING OF BIRDS, GAMBOLING OF LAMBS — EVERYTHING REALLY.

Now the Coordinator recognizes the whole phrase. It is a quotation from *The Song of Solomon* (ii. 11,12): "For lo, the winter is past, the rain is over and gone; the flowers appear on the earth; the time of the singing of birds is come, and the voice of the turtle is heard in our land."

Such a cross-correspondence could be continued for a number of sessions. The main point with such an experiment is that neither group should see the other's notes and neither, of course, know what quotation to expect.

If the Coordinator selects a quotation beforehand, and the Spokespersons ask that "the continuing message be the one being thought of by So-and-so, our Coordinator," then it makes his or her job a lot easier when searching through the materials. However, in this case there is always the possibility of E.S.P. between the Coordinator and someone in each of the groups rather than in actual spirit contact. To have no one know what the quotation will be beforehand, though tougher on the Coordinator, is much more convincing.

Solitary Use

Can the talking board be used by just one person or does it have to have two participants or more? Certainly to start with you need at least two. I would even suggest your very first encounters be with four, five or six. You'll give far more energy to the spirit trying to come through and get more satisfying results, as I've already mentioned.

But when you have dealt with it as a group for a while, and have a good feel for what is happening, there is no reason why you shouldn't cut down. Some people seem to naturally work well together. If you find you are in wonderful harmony with a particular person, certainly try some talking board work with just the two of you. If this goes well, then you can each try working alone. But ease into this.

After you have been sitting at the board together for a while, have one of you sit back and leave the other to handle the planchette alone. You can even lead up to this by one person gently lifting their fingers from the planchette as it is moving, leaving just the other person's fingers there. Many times this will cause the board to immediately stop. If so, replace the missing hand and continue before trying again later.

Eventually there will come a point where the planchette, although it may slow considerably, will still keep moving with only the one hand on it. Keep on with this and you will find — just like first starting with a group — the board will seem to gain confidence, and power, and build up speed once more. Then you can continue from that point working alone, right from the start of a sitting.

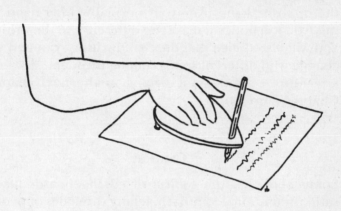

Pencil Planchette

Pencil Planchette

There is a way of using the planchette as a platform for automatic writing (which I will be dealing with more fully in the next chapter). Instead of having a leg, or support, under the pointed end of the moving platform, you drill a hole through and insert a pencil, or ballpoint pen. The point of the pen serves as the third foot for the planchette. With the platform resting on a large sheet of paper, any movement of it will cause the pen to leave a line on that paper. With a group of people sitting around the table, resting their fingers on the planchette in the center, as with the talking board, it is possible to get the pen to literally write out its messages as it moves around.

This arrangement especially lends itself to one person operation. With just one hand resting lightly on the platform, the planchette will move around and spell out messages or "converse" with you. It is interesting to use the opposite hand from your normal writing hand for this; you will notice it makes no difference to the writing. You will also notice that the "handwriting" can and will change with different spirits coming through.

More on automatic writing in the next chapter, Chapter Thirteen.

Caution

Some books on the subject of talking boards take a rather sensational approach, telling dire tales of people — usually very young or very old people — who have been sadly led astray by the messages received. They tell of young teenagers who have asked the board when they will die, only to be told that it will happen that following year! Needless to say this can have a terrible psychological effect on the recipient of such news. But this only points up the fact that the talking board is not a toy; it is a tool.

There are certain precautions that you need to take when using this, as with any tool. First of all, if you start getting a lot of negative messages, particularly messages telling you to do certain things that go against your grain, that you would not normally consider doing, then *stop using the board!* It's as simple as that.

If "the board" tells you to give away all your worldly wealth . . . stop and think about it! Who is telling you to do this, and why? It may be a spirit claiming to be Jesus or one of the Angels . . . but what is the likelihood? And why, if they are who they claim to be, would they tell you to do something that would leave you in dire straits? Don't quit your job on the advice of a long-dead relative, or a character from hundreds of years ago. What would they know about today's labor market? How conversant would your great-grandfather be with, say, modern computer science?

In other words, use your head. Don't run to the talking board expecting to get answers to all your problems. The spirits don't necessarily have the answers, they cannot see into the future, and they may be the last persons to give you good advice.

In marketing the Ouija board, the phrase "mystifying Oracle" is used. This implies that the board is able to see into the future. Here is where that teenager put so much store in the misinformation that she was soon to die. The board is not an oracle; it cannot tell you of the future. But, use it with common sense; use it taking the precautions that I have outlined; use it and don't abuse it, and you will have no problems. Far from it, you will gain a lot of enjoyment.

XIII

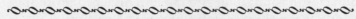

AUTOMATIC WRITING

The Hand that Writes by Itself

Automatic writing is that which is performed without the use of the conscious mind. That is, writing that is performed by the unconscious muscular energies of the hand and arm. Yet you cannot use those muscles to write without some direction governing what is being written. The "director" of automatic writing — the one whose brain is being used — is the spirit with whom you are in contact.

In practice what happens is that you take up a pencil, or pen, and hold it over a large sheet of paper. You then direct your attention elsewhere. In a short time your hand starts to make small movements, seemingly of its own volition. These movements cause marks to be made on the paper. As time goes on these marks become more and more consistent and consecutive. They begin to form circles, hooks, etc., until letters, then words, and finally whole sentences are written out.

One of the joys of automatic writing is that it can be done virtually anywhere. It can be done while reading a book, watching television, or even while talking to someone on the telephone. Just seat yourself comfortably where you can have a sheet of paper beside you with your hand, and pen, resting on the paper. I would suggest first doing your cleansing and protection exercises, to set up your barriers. You can even go so far as to make contact with your guide and ask him or her to invite spirits in to make contact with you through writing.

Then get into whatever it is you will be doing: reading, watching television, or whatever. And here is one form of spiritual contact where you do want to be absorbed in something else entirely, at least for the first dozen or so times you do this. You see, if you just sit and concentrate on your hand and pen, your own conscious mind will come into play. You may start to write but you are just as likely to be writing something which you are directing, rather than allowing a spirit to come in and communicate. So better by far to project your attention elsewhere and leave the spirit to its own devices for a while.

Automatic Writing while Engaged in Conversation

Try to forget that you are holding the pen. Once your hand starts to move you will have an almost irresistible urge to look down and see what is being written. But do resist it. Get absorbed in whatever you are doing and let your hand do its thing. You will find that it will move very slowly at first but will gradually move faster. Once the spirit has adjusted to your muscle power the hand will start to move very rapidly. In fact, once you get going your hand will just fly across the page, writing far faster than you would be able to do normally. For this reason I say use a large sheet, or pad, of paper. When you get to the bottom of the page you will certainly need to glance down enough to turn the page of the pad. What I have done in the past, and found to be very useful, is to sit at a table and have a large sheet of artist's paper (the back of rolls of wallpaper is ideal, too) spread out so that I can write a tremendous amount without having to pause to turn a page, or interfere in any way.

It helps if you hold your arm clear of the table. That is, so that neither the wrist nor elbow touches it. In this way a certain amount of fatigue will occur, which seems to help induce the writing.

Don't Try to Direct

Be careful to separate your mind from the actions of your hand and arm. Do not in any way try to direct what is being written. If you had the discipline you could certainly sit and just let the spirit take charge and write, and you could watch what was being written as it happened. In fact I will talk about doing just that a little later on. But, for now, few of us have that much discipline that we can sit and not influence what is being written. You would see something and think, however briefly perhaps,

"Oh, it's going to say so-and-so." Sure enough it would say "so-and-so." But it might have done so simply because of your influence. Perhaps it had been about to write something quite different. So, at least until you really get used to the action of automatic writing, and can really keep your own mind apart, just absorb yourself in some other activity so that the spirit can have free rein.

Some people obtain the writing more easily if they hold the pen or pencil between the first and second fingers, like a cigarette. This is different from the normal way of holding a writing instrument and helps in not forcing the writing in any way. But you don't have to hold it like this. Do whatever feels most comfortable and allows you to temporarily forget that you are holding anything.

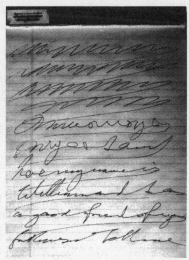

Sample of Automatic Writing

You will sometimes find that to start with you are not really getting writing, in the sense of actual letters and words. Sometimes the pen will go scribbling across the page, line after line, and when you later study it you find there is nothing there but scribble. This may even happen for the first two or three times you try automatic writing. Don't be discouraged. Eventually the scribble will form into words. What is happening is that the spirit communicating is simply getting the feel of your muscles and familiarizing him or herself enough to be able to write. Usually when there is this long preliminary to the actual writing, when the writing finally comes it is especially striking, both in its content and its length.

Types of Messages

What sort of things will be written? One automatist read what had been written and found it was by a man calling himself James Valentine. He said that he had just recently (a few hours earlier) been killed in a railroad accident and gave the details: time and place. On later checking, the automatist found everything to be accurate; a James Valentine had indeed been killed at the time and place stated. The man had been driving his car across an unguarded railroad crossing when the vehicle stalled out. He sat there and tried to restart the car, thinking he could make it before the oncoming locomotive reached him. He left it too long.

It's not common to make immediate contact with such a person; one newly dead. You are far more likely to be contacted by a deceased relative or friend. Or someone whom you did not know when alive but who has a special interest in you.

One of the especially interesting things that can happen is that you will find the handwriting is not your own! In fact, when you get messages from a number of different spirits you will frequently find that each has his or her own handwriting, as they had when alive. A Mrs. Grace Rosher worked with a pen propped lightly against her fingers and quickly found herself getting long communications in a strange hand. The spirit signed the messages "William Crookes." It was later verified that the handwriting was in fact that of the late Sir William Crookes, the pioneer parapsychologist!

Check What You Receive

As with all spiritual contact, carefully check the material your receive. Make note of all names, dates and places. Try to verify what you are told. Only in this way will you be able to assure yourself (let alone anyone else) that you are indeed in contact with the spirit world, the Second Level.

When you have been receiving for a while — about a dozen or so separate occasions, at least — then you can start to respond directly to what you are receiving. You can read what has been written and then, consciously writing yourself, write out a question. Giving up control again, wait for the answer to come from spirit. In this way you can get into a conversation with the spirit. The trick, of course, is to be able to give up conscious control and let the arm/hand/pen go free, so that you get unadulterated responses to your questions.

Either Hand

Another way to ensure that what you get is not coming from you, is to use the other hand from the one you normally use for writing. If you are normally right-handed, hold the pen in your left hand for automatic writing, and vice versa. In fact, when you get into "conversation," you can have your left hand write for the spirit and ask your questions through your normal right hand! It will take longer for the spirits to adjust to writing through you this way, however. The reason is simply that you are not used to moving your hand and manipulating your wrist for writing with that hand and so spirit will have to work harder to get it as supple as the hand you normally use. But, again, persevere and you'll get great results.

William Stainton Moses

William Stainton Moses (1839-1892), probably the greatest physical medium after D. D. Home, produced a great number of automatic writings, from various spirits, which were published under the title *Spirit Teachings*. Of his writing, Moses said:

> *At first the writing was slow and it was necessary for me to follow it with my eye, but even then the thoughts were not my thoughts. Very soon all the messages assumed a character of which I had no doubt whatever that the thought opposed my own.*

But I cultivated the power of occupying my mind
with other things during the time that the writing
was going on, and was able to read an abstruse
book and follow out a line of close reasoning, while
the message was written with unbroken regularity.
Messages so written extended over many pages and
in their course there is no correction, no fault in
composition, and often a sustained vigour and
beauty of style.

William T. Stead (1849-1912) was another excellent
automatist. He was a British journalist in the late nineteenth century who became interested in automatic writing and received many messages from the spirits of dead
friends. Later he went on to another unique aspect of
automatic writing . . . he started receiving messages from
living friends! He would write out a question addressed
to someone he knew and after a few moments his hand
would write out the response. In this way he came into
possession of a great deal of information not previously
known to him yet vouched for by the friends who "wrote"
it! An interesting sidelight on William Stead is that he
had repeated dreams and visions of a giant ocean liner
being sunk by an iceberg in the Atlantic Ocean. He
wrote about this and about the number of lives that
could be lost if there was a shortage of lifeboats. Twenty-
six years later he was himself to go down with the *Titanic*.

Character of the Messages Received

Many of the messages you receive, especially at first, will
seem incoherent and disconnected, almost like dreams.
In fact they may be dreams. When you first start you may
be able to disassociate your mind from the page, yet your
unconscious may still be tenaciously clinging on to the

point where it intrudes on what is written. It may be your dream consciousness (or subconscious) which is originating the messages.

The only way to work this out is through your meditation before you start, by aids such as affirmations, and by engrossing yourself as deeply as possible in some other activity when you start. Working a crossword puzzle or solving mathematical equations, rather than just watching television, are good deep-rooting activities to start with, if you feel your unconscious is intruding.

Some people find it helps — as with many types of spirit communication — to sit in a darkened room when first trying automatic writing. If you have no luck in full light then certainly try this in varying degrees of darkness.

Patience Worth

In the earlier part of this century a St. Louis housewife encountered a spirit named Patience Worth. Mrs. Pearl Curran was persuaded by a friend, Emily Hutchinson, to use a Ouija board (see Chapter Twelve). Although not particularly interested, Mrs. Curran agreed and worked the board with her friend a number of times. On the evening of July 8, 1913, the planchette started spelling out a message that read: "Many moons ago I lived. Again I come; Patience Worth my name."

The spirit identified herself as a seventeenth century Englishwoman who had lived in the county of Dorset. She said that she was a spinster and that she later emigrated to America and was finally killed by Indians. The two women, Curran and Hutchinson, started speaking with Patience Worth on a regular basis. Then they found that Mrs. Curran could contact her by herself, whereas Mrs. Hutchinson had no luck alone.

From the Ouija board Pearl Curran went on to automatic writing and, through that, ended up producing 2500 poems, short stories, plays, allegories and six full-length novels, all authored by Patience Worth! She produced a total of over four million words within a period of five years.

What is especially interesting about the Patience Worth case is that Pearl Curran had dropped out of school at the age of fourteen and had virtually no knowledge of life in the mid-sixteen hundreds, either in England or the American colonies. Yet experts have examined the writings produced, have not found a single anachronism and have found revealed an amazing insight into the life and times of that period. The vocabulary had an incredibly high ninety percent of Old English in it. This is probably one of the best recorded examples ever of spirit contact. The writings continued through from 1913 to the late 1920s. Mrs. Pearl Curran died in 1937.

Inspirational Writing

Another form of automatic writing, known as *inspirational writing,* is where you study what you are writing as you write it. Although you do not set out to write anything in particular, you find that the words form in your head — rather than directly onto the paper — and you write what seems to be inspired. This can be a form of spirit communication in that the spirit may be coming through your head, rather than directly to the muscles of your arm, but it is far more likely that what you write is influenced by your own thoughts and feelings. It is not "pure" spiritual writing; or is unlikely to be. What you produce is probably a mixture from your own unconscious and from your Higher Self.

Great Composers Return

In 1964 Rosemary Brown, a widowed housewife in Balham, London, struggling to bring up two children, began to write music that she claimed was actually written through her by the spirits of Liszt, Schubert, Chopin, Brahms, Bach, Rachmaninoff, Debussy, Stravinsky and Beethoven. She does not play the piano well enough to play most of the music she is receiving, yet she has been observed writing out the manuscripts at a tremendous speed. Pianist Hephzibah Menuhin said: "I look at these manuscripts with immense respect. Each piece is distinctly in the composer's style." Composer Richard Rodney Bennet said: "A lot of people can improvise, but you can't fake music like this without years of training." In 1970 a recording was issued *(Rosemary Brown's Music)* with Rosemary Brown struggling through some of the pieces on one side of the record, and concert pianist Peter Katin playing the more difficult pieces on the other side.

Automatic Art

Although automatic writing is the best known, and most common, of the automatisms, there are also many instances of pictures being drawn and paintings being painted by mediums. A housewife in Michigan, with no artistic training, suddenly started drawing and painting beautiful pictures. Her unusual method was to start at one side of the paper or canvas and work her way across to the other side, doing all the details of the picture as she went. It was like peeling back a top cover to reveal the picture beneath. She claimed that it was dead artists who worked through her.

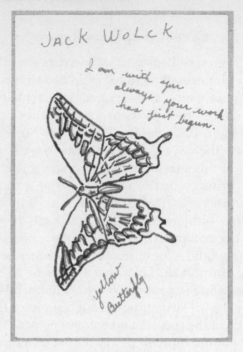

JACK WOLCK

I am with you always. your work has just begun.

yellow Butterfly

Automatic Art
(John G. Wolck)

In 1905 another untrained artist, Frederic Thompson, started painting in the style of the dead painter Robert Swain Gifford. Professor James Hyslop, the psychical researcher, was so impressed he reported the case in his book, *Contact With the Other World*.

If you feel so inclined you can ask your Spirit Guide to bring artists through you, in doing automatic communication. Let your hand roam freely as you sketch; have colors available to paint; just let it happen. But, as with writing, check as far as you are able to find out who is coming through you. The artist may sign his or her work or you may have to haunt galleries and dig through art books to find the originator.

XIV

⊙•••⊙•••⊙•••⊙•••⊙•••⊙•••⊙•••⊙•••⊙•••⊙•••⊙•••⊙•••⊙•••⊙

Spirit Photography

Unexpected Visitors

Mr. and Mrs. Chinnery, of Ipswich, England, went to visit the grave of Mrs. Chinnery's mother. They laid some flowers there and turned to leave. As Mabel Chinnery lingered a moment, her husband got into their car. She turned and, on an impulse, took a photograph of her husband looking out of the car window at her. Then she too got into the car and they left. Some few days later Mabel Chinnery picked up the developed photographs from the store and took them home. Imagine her surprise when, on looking at the picture of her husband in the car, she saw her deceased mother sitting in the back seat!

This happened in 1959. The *London Sunday Pictorial* newspaper published the photograph, declaring it genuine after their photographic expert had examined it.

Can spirits of the dead be photographed? Obviously, from the above, they can. There are certainly many examples of ghosts — disembodied spirits — that have been photographed. One of the most frequently pictured is Dorothy Walpole, the so-called Brown Lady of Raynham Hall, in Norfolk, England. She appears from time to time, descending the staircase of the hall and has been photographed on several occasions.

Around the turn of the century there were any number of professed "spirit photographs" produced. They were usually pictures of sitters with an image of a deceased family member hovering in the background. It seems probable that virtually all of these were fraudulently produced, by double exposure or similar means. In those early days of photography there was also a lot of unconscious fraud brought about by poor developing, incorrect chemicals, light streaks, and the like. However, one or two were very carefully examined by photographic experts and proclaimed genuine.

William Mumler was the first to produce spirit photographs. He was an engraver who lived in Boston. In 1862 he tried to take a photograph of himself by focusing his camera on a chair, uncapping the lens, and then leaping into the picture to pose in the chair! Waiting a little too long, his first picture just showed the chair; the second the chair . . . and a young girl sitting in it. The figure was transparent and the girl seemed to fade away from the waist down. Mumler recognized her as a cousin who had died nearly twelve years before.

Some reports say that actually Mumler was photographing a Dr. Gardner when the figure of the girl appeared on one of the plates. Be that as it may, Mumler went on to make a name for himself as a spirit photographer, though most of his later pictures were of the fraudulent variety. However, on one occasion Mary Todd Lincoln, the President's widow, went to him under an assumed name. There was no way that Mumler could have known who she was, yet the developed photograph of her showed the late President standing at her side.

British Experiments

Spirit photography appeared in Britain a decade after it had stirred the hearts of spiritualists in America. A number of British mediums tried to get results without success. Finally the two respected mediums Mr. and Mrs. Samuel Guppy hired a photographer named Hudson and asked him to take pictures. Hudson took a picture of Samuel Guppy and the photograph revealed a faint, draped spirit-like form in the background. Further pictures showed other figures.

Hudson soon became very popular as a spirit photographer, and was intensively investigated by the spiritualist community. Thomas Slater, an optician by profession, and another professional photographer named Beattie — an out-and-out skeptic where spirit photography was concerned — gave Hudson a thorough examination. They subsequently issued the following statement:

> *They (the photographs) were not made by double exposure, nor by figures projected in space in any way; they were not the result of mirrors; they were not produced by any machinery in the background, behind it, above it, or below it, or by any contrivance connected with the bath, the camera, or the camera-slide.*

The editor of the *British Journal of Photography*, Traill Taylor, added that "at no time during the preparation, exposure, or development of the pictures was Mr. Hudson within ten feet of the camera or the dark room."

Repeatable Phenomena

It was not until 1962 that anyone seemed able to produce repeatable phenomena, and then it was in the form of thought photographs, rather than specifically spirit photographs. Using a Polaroid camera, Ted Serios produced an amazing array of pictures of anything he thought of. He would concentrate on a particular building, for example, point the camera at himself and click the shutter. The photograph that came out was of that building!

Serios would use anybody's camera, not just his own. He was thoroughly investigated, with people carefully marking their film before it was used and giving him the subject on which to concentrate. Curtis Fuller, President of the Illinois Society for Psychic Research, was the first man to bring Serios' achievements to the public eye. Dr. Jule Eisenbud then picked up on the man and did extensive studies over a period of four years, eventually writing a book on the subject (*The World of Ted Serios* Morrow, New York 1967). Not every single one of Ted Serios' pictures came out. Many were blank or just showed what the camera aimed at. But a tremendous number showed houses, people, street scenes, famous buildings . . . an incredible variety of verifiable pictures produced by his concentration alone.

Your Own Spirit Photographs

To preclude conscious fraud, the best thing is to take photographs yourself. And the best place to take them is right there in the room you use for your séances.

Polaroid Spirit Photograph of Subject's Mother
(John. G. Wolck)

Polaroid Spirit Photograph
(Barbara Wolck)

Set up a camera on a tripod, far enough back that it can take in the whole scene of you and your friend(s) around the table. Start as you normally do by establishing harmony, visualizing light, and grounding through singing and/or prayer. Then continue with either table-tipping or talking board, or whatever method you prefer to contact the spirits. (If you want to do everything alone, then do your meditation and go on to contacting your Guide and then the spirits.) When in contact, ask the spirit if he or she would be willing to appear in a photograph. Of course, willingness is no guarantee of appearance. You may take many photographs before you actually get an appearance. But, as with so much in spirit communication, perseverance is the keyword.

When the spirit agrees, move across to the camera and take the picture. Do not use flash. Use a fast speed film; I would recommend at least 400 ASA. You can get 1600 or even 2000 ASA film, if you hunt a little. This is ideal for use in very low light situations. And if you want to experiment a little more, get hold of some infrared film and take your pictures in the dark or near dark. You will probably go through a number of rolls of film, but there is no reason why you should not be successful.

From here go on to more direct portraiture. Get one member of your circle to sit in a chair, ready to be photographed. Again, ask your spirit to participate. Then simply take a picture of the person in the chair. There is a chance that you will find a second figure in the developed photograph.

The use of a Polaroid camera can give you immediate results, but a roll of 35mm or similar film is less expensive, since you will be taking a lot of pictures. Use as slow a shutter speed as you can. It seems that too fast a shutter speed does not always allow the spirit time to materialize on the film, though why that should be I do not know. I would recommend a speed of no faster than 1/30 second.

If one of your circle is able to go into trance, then photograph him or her that way. (Again let me stress, no flash.) Many of the earlier pictures of spirits were taken with the camera focused on an entranced medium.

Photographs Without a Camera

An experiment was carried out in 1932, in Los Angeles. A number of scientists were present and were subsequently able to reproduce the results.

They gathered together in a photographic darkroom. The only light was the red safelight, normally used in the darkroom. To double-check that there was no light intrusion of any sort, sheets of unexposed photographic paper were put down on the floor all around the room. If there was any extraneous light it would show up on one or more of those, afterwards.

Sheets of similarly sensitized photographic paper were cut into strips about two inches wide and passed out to the scientists. They were instructed to hold the strip by the ends, across their foreheads, bowed out so that it did not actually contact the skin. The sensitive side was towards their skin. Holding the strips of paper in this fashion, the scientists then concentrated their thoughts on various objects of their own choosing. For example, one would concentrate on a person, another on a building, another on a flower or bird. After a period of this intense concentration all the paper was gathered up and processed.

None of the sheets scattered around the floor produced anything, showing that there was no light seepage of any sort. But of the strips, several developed actual pictures corresponding to the image that the holder had thought.

Many Experiments

You might try a variation on the above. In a darkroom you could load up squares of photographic paper in small light-restricting envelopes (or wrap them carefully in aluminum foil). Then bring them out into the séance room and pass them out to the sitters, where they could hold them to their foreheads. This would save everyone from having to squeeze into a darkroom.

Another variation would be for everyone to concentrate their thoughts (of the same object) onto one square of paper in the center of the table. Or, hold hands around the table and ask the spirit to cause its image to appear on the sheet lying on the table.

Put up a movie/slide projection screen and have everyone concentrate their thoughts; projecting an image onto that screen, all thinking of the same thing, of course. Then take a photograph of the blank screen.

Try the same thing but using a dark sheet, rather than the white screen. Sometimes it seems it is easier for the spirits to come through on one type of background and sometimes on another. Remember to try both regular film and infrared.

Do not forget to keep notes on everything you try. This is especially important with photography, so that you might duplicate what is successful. Note the type of film used, its ASA rating, the aperture and speed, and the type and amount of lighting you had. Note also the number of people both present and concentrating, proportion of males to females, positions, and distances from camera/screen.

XV

PHYSICAL MEDIUMS

In mental mediumship the medium communicates through clairvoyance, clairaudience, clairsentience, direct speech, crystal-gazing or scrying, and so on, as we have seen. Physical mediums are those who levitate, who bring apports, create rappings, produce the sound of bells and musical instruments, move objects, exhibit transfiguration and, in short, interfere with a physical, material object without using any part of their body in a way that would normally explain the interference.

If a heavy table, on the far side of the room from where the medium and everyone else is sitting, should slowly rise up off the floor, hang suspended for a few moments, then gently settle down again, this would be classed as physical phenomena. And it has been known to happen!

Physical spiritualist phenomena is of the sort that we have been taught, all our lives, cannot happen; it goes against the laws of physics. It goes, frequently, against the law of gravity. Yet what we should really be saying is that all this goes against these laws *as we know them today*. It is, perhaps, presumptuous of us to believe that we know all there is to know. Obviously if we did we would have no further need for scientists of any sort.

Perhaps the best introduction to physical mediumship is to look closely at one of the greatest physical mediums of all times and what she could achieve. I have previously mentioned Eusapia Paladino; she was certainly one of the greats. It is also true that she was caught in fraud a number of times, but I'll look at that aspect in a moment.

Eusapia Paladino

Eusapia was a rough peasant girl from southern Italy. She was crude, chthonic and uneducated and never tried in the least to become cultured or genteel, often to the embarrassment of her sponsors and investigators. She was illiterate, yet she had a great understanding of human nature.

In *The Unknown — Is It Nearer?* (Signet Books 1956) authors Dingwall and Langdon-Davies say of her:

> *She cheated whenever she could. She cheated in England and she cheated in America. Whenever she found herself investigated by men so incompetent at their job that cheating was easy, she cheated. In England she was detested for her bad manners and worse morals, and in America the ballyhoo atmosphere was such that no genuine psi phenomena could have been expected. Eusapia quite bluntly paid her hosts out in both countries for grossly mismanaging their duties as serious researchers into paranormal phenomena.*

Yet when subjected to stringent controls by researchers who knew their job, Eusapia was a psychic investigator's dream. A wonderful example is to be found in the investigation conducted by three researchers from the Society of Psychical Research in London. Those men were Hereward Carrington, W. W.

Eusapia Paladino

Baggally and Everard Feilding. To again quote Dingwall and Langdon-Davies: ". . . (the) investigation was carried out by men so competent that we have to accept their word for what they saw, and what they saw was inexplicable in terms of fraud."

Carrington had spent many years exposing fraudulent mediums and probably knew every trick in the book. He was a prolific writer on parapsychology and became the founder of the American Psychical Institute and Laboratory. Baggally did not believe in psychic phenomena at all and more of a skeptic would have been hard to find. Yet he had been puzzled and fascinated by some of Eusapia's previous demonstrations and very much wanted to investigate further. Both Carrington and Baggally, as well as being competent investigators, were also accomplished amateur conjurers fully versed in most mediumistic-type tricks. Feilding was the Honorary

Secretary of the Society for Psychical Research. He did an exhaustive investigation of the materialization medium Florence Cook.

The three investigators started by hanging two thin black curtains across a corner of the room, at Eusapia's request. This formed what is generally known as a "cabinet" for the medium and is a common requisite. Some mediums actually sit inside this cabinet, though others sit outside it. Behind this curtain was placed a small round table with various objects on it: a trumpet, a bell, tambourine, toy piano, whistle, and other odds and ends. The medium didn't look behind the curtain and had no way of knowing exactly what was there.

With the three investigators, Eusapia sat at a small oblong table, her back to the cabinet and about two feet from it. There was an investigator on either side of her holding her hands and controlling her feet and legs, by keeping their feet on hers and their legs pressed against hers. Additionally, the third investigator would sometimes actually get down on the floor underneath the table to make sure she was not cheating in any way. There was low light but it was, as Feilding reported, "bright enough to enable us to read small print."

The phenomena Eusapia produced included the levitation of the oblong table, which would rise up in the air a good two feet, remain suspended for a few moments, and then settle back down again. Frequently her hands were held by the others at a distance from the table, so that she was not in contact with it in any way. These levitations occurred in full light. The table would also rock up to stand on two legs. The men would press down on it and it would pop up again as though suspended on elastic cords!

Photograph of the Table Resting on the Floor

Photograph of the Same Table Raised to a Height of Twenty-Five Centimeters (Photos by M. G. de Fontenay)

*Complete Leviation of a Table in Professor Flammarion's Salon
through Mediumship of Eusapia Paladino*

When in lower light, although the men carefully
kept hold of the medium, they felt themselves frequently being touched on the arms, shoulders and
head. Then, apparently living hands — they could feel
the fingers and even the nails — would grasp at them
through the curtains. It was the sort of thing that they
would have thought could only have been done by an
accomplice behind the curtains . . . yet there was no one
else in the room and certainly no space for anyone
behind the curtains!

Suddenly the small table from inside the cabinet
was projected out through the curtains and landed with
its top against the oblong table, its legs pointing back
towards the cabinet. Again in Feilding's words: "It would
appear to hang there and try to climb on our table,

which it never succeeded in doing." Then the objects that had been on the small table came rushing out:

> *The flageolet tapped me on the head, the tambourine jumped on my lap, the tea-bell was rung and presently appeared, ringing, over Eusapia's head, carried by a hand which attached it quickly to her hair, reappeared, detached the bell itself, rang it again over Eusapia's head and threw it onto the séance table.*

While all this was occurring Feilding was holding one of Eusapia's hands close to his face and Baggally was holding the other. Apparently there was sufficient light for a secretary, also present and sitting about eight feet away, to take notes in shorthand. A stool started to move and the secretary passed his hands around it but found no hidden strings or wires. It still continued to move.

Drawing from Photograph Showing Method of Control by Professors Lombroso and Richet of Eusapia — Table Completely Raised

Such were the phenomena produced by an extremely accomplished physical medium when she really got serious about it!

An equally accomplished physical medium was Daniel Dunglas Home, whom I mentioned in Chapter Four. Home was also examined on many occasions by investigators, whose credentials were impeccable, and found to be authentic. Unlike Eusapia, Home was never caught cheating. But, sadly, for every Paladino and Home there were, and are, hundreds of frauds. So much so that physical mediums as a whole have a terrible reputation and are seldom taken seriously. Perhaps this is why there are so few of them around today?

Spirits Take Charge

The phenomena produced by the likes of Eusapia Paladino are certainly impressive, but what bearing do they have on spirit communication and the survival of bodily death?

At most séances where a physical medium is present there is a tie-in between what is produced, by way of phenomena, and contact with the Second Level. It is usually a spirit who has been contacted who is responsible for the movement of the objects or the touching of hands, etc.

The séance usually starts in the normal way with contact being made with the medium's guide and then contact with a sought-after deceased relative or friend of one of the sitters. The difference between the mental and physical medium then shows itself in that rather than the medium relaying the spirit's words and actions, the spirit actually takes charge and produces evidence of being present.

One of the tools of the physical medium is the trumpet. This is a light, metal cone much like a megaphone. Frequently it is painted with luminous paint, either entirely or just around the rim of mouthpiece and bell. This way any movement of the trumpet can be observed, even in a darkened séance room.

The trumpet is placed in the center of the circle. At some point it rises up and floats around the circle. It will eventually stop in front of one of the sitters and the voice of the spirit may be heard coming out of it. Usually the voice is of such volume and quality that the sitter has no trouble in recognizing who is speaking. Apparently the trumpet can in this way serve to amplify the spirit's voice, to the point where it can be heard directly by the sitter.

Tiny spots of light are also frequently seen floating about the circle and dancing around the sitters. These are often associated with the deceased, as their way of showing that they are indeed present.

Transfiguration

Sometimes when the spirit speaks through the medium, not only will its voice be quite recognizable but the medium's face will assume the characteristics of the spirit's face. A young female medium may suddenly assume the appearance of an old man; a clean-shaven older man may seem to get younger and grow a moustache! A very notable transfiguration can take place with a good physical medium.

I have personally seen an older woman shed all the little lines, the "crow's feet" and bags under the eyes, to look like a young woman of about eighteen. It is striking the first time you see it.

On the other hand, I have also seen an older male medium who professed to change into about fifteen different characters. He worked in a red light, which was set down on the ground. In this way, by simply tipping back his head slightly a shadow was produced on his upper lip which gave the appearance of a moustache! For the rest, I'll just say it was unimpressive and there was no way I would have believed the spirits were present. Yet, it is amazing how gullible people can be; how very much some people want to believe. Of the sitters who were present, the majority were totally caught up in what they saw as incredible transformations. Some even saw extra characters, including John Kennedy and other notables! Perhaps I was at fault . . . perhaps they really were there but I didn't see them.

Ectoplasm and Materialization

Another of the psychic "tools," if I can call them that, of the physical medium is a strange substance known as *ectoplasm* (from the Greek *ektos* and *plasma;* "exteriorized substance"). This is a white substance that exudes from the various bodily orifices of the medium. It varies in intensity from a fine mist to a solidity that can be felt and which can move objects. It has an odor peculiar to itself, which has been described by sitters as reminding them of ozone.

According to Foster Damon of Harvard University, the philosopher Vaughan described ectoplasm back in the seventeenth century, though he referred to it then as "first matter" drawn from the body.

Ectoplasm is sensitive to light so few photographs had been taken of it, until recently with the use of infrared pictures. There are some excellent photos of the British medium Jack Webber, taken at a séance in the 1930s. They show lengths of ectoplasm coming from his mouth and from his navel. Each supports a trumpet in midair. Webber himself is seated in a chair with his arms and legs tied securely to those of the chair. Other pictures show a table being lifted by an ectoplasmic rod coming from the medium.

Jack Webber Exuding Ectoplasm
(Photo Courtesy Psychic Press)

Ectoplasm will form into the likeness of spirits' faces, even full figures. Sometimes it becomes a hand and the hand is felt by the sitters. Gustav Geley, the distinguished modern psychic researcher, described how a misty column of the substance formed beside him at one séance then, out of the middle of it, came a hand which gradually became more and more solid. Finally the hand reached out and touched him on the arm. He described it as a friendly pat and the hand as being icy cold.

The fascinating, and non-professional, medium Elizabeth d'Esperance (1855-1919) produced some amazing materializations out of ectoplasm. Once, when at the house of a professor and circle of friends, an extremely beautiful young woman materialized. Elizabeth d'Esperance was sitting in the open, outside the cabinet, when it happened. The young figure dipped her hand into a paraffin bucket and left an impression that was later cast as a plaster mold. It was described as a hand of "rare beauty." What was especially surprising was that an expert claimed it to be normally impossible to extricate one's hand from the paraffin without ruining the mold. While materialized, the beautiful young woman wrote in a notebook provided by one of the sitters. What she wrote no one present could read. It turned out to be in ancient Greek and, when translated, said: "I am Nepenthes thy friend; when thy soul is oppressed by too much pain, call on me, Nepenthes, and I will come at once to relieve thy trouble."

Many were the fraudulent mediums who tried to hoodwink the public by producing "ectoplasm" which turned out to be gauze or cheesecloth, sometimes wadded up and held in the mouth. However, none could duplicate some of the exudations photographed (sometimes without the medium's knowledge) by infrared where the ectoplasm is seen emerging from the ears, nose, navel, breasts, etc., of the medium. And having emerged and been used to show contact with the spirit(s), the substance will then retract back into the medium's body.

Some mediums have been weighed, or placed on a scale throughout the séance. It has been found that they can lose as much as fifty percent of their weight when producing ectoplasm!

I have mentioned that ectoplasm is sensitive to light. Many mediums have been injured when there has been a sudden flash of light, unexpected and unannounced. It is as though the ectoplasm "snaps back" into the medium like a rubber band. Franek Kluski, the Polish medium, was badly cut from such a sudden, unexpected retraction; Evan Powell, in London, at the British College of Psychic Science, suffered a bad chest injury; George Valiantine had a large bruise for several days after a flash of light caused his ectoplasm to spring back.

Apports

Sometimes the spirits wish to bring a gift to a sitter and an actual, physical object will materialize in the séance room. This is known as an *apport* (from the French *apporter,* "to bring"). It might be something as small and seemingly insignificant as a tiny pebble, or it might be a flower, or an expensive piece of jewelry or statuary. Size and weight seem not to matter. Huge blocks of ice have been apported as have tremendously big sunflowers, complete with clumped soil around the roots. The fact that the object has materialized from out of thin air, as it were, is sensational enough whatever its form, I feel.

Sometimes the apport comes flying through the air and hits the face of the sitter before falling onto the table. Sometimes it strikes the table first, with force. Other times it simply appears there. Apports as strange as live lobsters have appeared in séance rooms! One of the most common forms of apports is for all the sitters to be sprayed with perfume.

Apports can be animate or inanimate. There have been innumerable instances of birds appearing. One famous case occurred in Boston in the early years of American spiritualism. "The Olive Branch of Peace Circle" had been advised, by spirit, that there would be such an apport. To safeguard against fraud the séance room was hermetically sealed for twenty-four hours before the séance. Yet, on cue, a white dove appeared and flew quietly around the room.

The opposite of an apport is an *asport;* when an object disappears from the séance room and is sent to a destination outside.

The two main theories regarding apports are that the object is brought from a fourth dimension, or that it is somehow disintegrated where it previously existed and reintegrated into the séance room, à la the "transporter" of *Star Trek* fame. This latter theory seems to be supported by the fact that many apports are hot to the touch when they first arrive, and a thermic reaction would certainly be expected with the law of transmutation of energy.

A spirit named White Hawk explained the phenomenon this way: "I speed up the atomic vibrations until the (objects) are disintegrated. Then they are brought here and I slow down the vibrations until they become solid again."

The most interesting, and possibly most humorous, case of an apport was that of Mrs. Samuel Guppy. Mrs. Guppy was herself famous for her apports, but in this instance she became an apport! The séance was being held at 69 Lamb's Conduit Street in London, by two mediums: Charles Williams and Frank Herne. There were eight sitters present.

The circle was in contact with a Katie King (who claimed to be the famous guide, by that name, of medium Florence Cook). When the spirit offered to bring an apport one of the sitters, jokingly, suggested she bring Mrs. Guppy . . . Mrs. Guppy was a very large lady! Everyone was laughing at the suggestion when, with a loud thump, the figure of a woman appeared in the middle of the table. It was Mrs. Guppy!

Mrs. Guppy lived more than three miles away, in Highbury. Witnesses attested to the fact that she was sitting in her study doing her accounts. Indeed, when she arrived on the séance table — looking very puzzled — she was holding a pen still wet with ink! One of the sitters was the editor of *The Spiritualist*. He and two others accompanied Mrs. Guppy back home, where there were assured by members of her household that only recently the lady had been seen working in her study.

Developing Physical Mediumship

The development of physical mediumship is usually much slower than that of mental mediumship. It requires a lot of patience. It is also something which lends itself more to personal, solitary development, whereas mental mediumship can readily flourish in a group setting and through circle development (see Chapter Seventeen).

Several physical mediums have spoken of feeling a "cobwebby" sensation, like very fine threads, when physical phenomena are about to materialize. Elizabeth d'Esperance said, "My first impression is of being covered with spider webs . . . It seemed that I could feel fine threads being drawn out of the pores of my skin." You might also feel the sensation of being touched on various parts of your body. These are signs of physical power being present and can occur when you are meditating or doing affirmations.

When you speak with your guide, or Doorkeeper, you should ask that you be able to bring out any physical power, if you are inclined that way. Then, look for it; try to be aware of it if it comes. Don't let yourself be totally distracted from whatever else you are doing — clairvoyance, scrying, billet reading — but, should you become aware of the "cobwebby" feeling, let it come through.

This isn't to say that you are necessarily going to produce ectoplasm; few mediums seem to have developed that capability today. But you may well be led into direct voice, psychokinesis (moving objects without physical contact), apports, or the like. Direct voice and transfiguration seem the most common of the physical phenomena, to begin with.

If you are doing clairvoyance and clairaudience, and can see your spirit contact clearly and can see/hear what they have to say, ask them if they will try to speak through you in direct voice. One way for this to happen is for the spirit to actually use your voice box. Another way is for them to construct a voice box out of ectoplasm, and speak using that.

Always have a trumpet in your circle, whether you feel you can produce direct voice or not. You can buy plastic megaphones which work well, though metal ones do seem preferable and certainly are more traditional. These can be made fairly easily, by bending a piece of tin into a cone shape. Just stand the trumpet in the middle of the circle — on the floor or the table — and forget it. It may be there every time you meet and never get used, but one day you just may be surprised when it is used.

XVI

HEALING

Spiritual Healing

Healing both the physically and the mentally sick can be done using the energies of the spirit world operating through a medium. It is not the same thing as a faith cure in that many people have been spiritually cured even when they had no belief that it could be done. Rather than depend upon the power of the individual's mind, operating consciously or unconsciously, spiritual healing utilizes the power and knowledge of the Second Level channeled through to this level by the medium.

Spiritual healing can be done in the following ways:

1. By the spiritual influences working directly through the body of the medium.

2. By the spiritual influences illuminating the brain of the medium, and thereby intensifying perception so that the seat of the disease becomes known, along with the remedy (as was done by Edgar Cayce).

3. Through the application of absent treatments, whereby spiritual beings combine their own healing forces with that of the medium and convey them to the (distant) patient, causing them to be absorbed by the system of that patient.

Obviously these definitions cover not only the facts of spiritual healing but also absent treatments and diagnosis.

Edgar Cayce

Edgar Cayce (1877-1945) practiced healing for forty-three years. He had never studied medicine; in fact, his education didn't extend beyond grammar school. Yet he was able to diagnose illnesses — either with a patient present or thousands of miles away — and to prescribe medicines and treatments which cured.

Cayce had exhibited psychic powers from a very young age, but his ability to channel curative energy didn't show up until he was twenty-one. At that time he suffered from very bad laryngitis. Unable to find a doctor who could help, he went to a hypnotist. In trance, Cayce himself came up with his own diagnosis and the cure. The hypnotist, Al Layne, then suggested they try to do the same thing for other people with medical problems. Although Cayce was dubious he agreed to try. He was amazingly successful. Over the period of forty-three years he went on to diagnose and prescribe for approximately thirty thousand people. All he needed in order to focus in on them was their name and address. Happily, records were kept of all the readings he did so that even today we are able to treat people according to Cayce's channeled prescriptions.

From working with Layne, Cayce went on to self-hypnotize — to put himself into trance — so that he was able to work alone. Through the material he channeled he came to believe strongly in reincarnation; something in which he did not believe initially.

One doctor, who worked with Cayce for some years, said of him:

> *His psychological terms and descriptions of the nervous anatomy would do credit to any professor of nervous anatomy. There is no faltering in his speech and all his statements are clear and concise. He handles the most complex "jawbreakers" with as much ease as any Boston physician, which to me is quite wonderful in view of the fact that while in his normal state he is an illiterate man, especially along the line of medicine, surgery or pharmacy, of which he knows nothing.*

But typically the medical community dismissed Cayce's work, turning a blind eye to the volume and the incredibly high success rate of his cures. Although today the majority still insist on wearing blinders, some few doctors in recent times have come to appreciate what he did and even work along similar lines.

When Cayce went into trance and considered a patient the first words he would say were always, "Yes, we can see the body;" a clue, I think, to the fact that it was spirit working through him. In his prescriptions he would sometimes include ingredients which had been long out of use. For example, one time he called for the use of balsam of sulfur. The pharmacist trying to fill the prescription had never heard of such a thing. It was only in looking back in a fifty-year-old pharmaceutical catalog that, by chance, he eventually found mention of balsam of sulfur. This is again, perhaps, indicative of the fact that working through him were spirits from the past.

Some British Spiritual Healers

Probably the best known spiritual healer in England was Harry Edwards (1893-1976). During World War I Edwards was working with some Arabs in the Middle East, building a railroad. In the course of the work many of the Arabs injured themselves and always went to Edwards to heal them. They referred to him as *hakim* — "healer." Edwards himself didn't think he was doing anything unusual, attributing their fast recovery to them rather than to himself. On returning to England, after the war, he did not trouble to pursue this. It was not until 1935 that he finally looked into spiritualism, and then it was a gradual "easing into" the healing side.

Edwards finally did come to recognize the fact that he was a good medium for healing. He never did think of himself as a healer, but simply as a channel for the energy. He had a great respect for the Native Americans, and their knowledge of herbs and healing, and for other similar cultures. He believed that it was Amerindians who worked through him. In later years he also came to recognize the channeled energies of Louis Pasteur and of Lord Lister. Many spiritualist healers do claim to have deceased doctors working through them.

My uncle, George Buckland — who was the person responsible for introducing me to the whole wonderful world of metaphysics, when I was about twelve — was a Spiritualist, and witnessed Harry Edwards' healings on many occasions. He would tell me of them and give his characteristic shrug and chuckle, saying it was impossible to believe what he had seen . . . and yet it happened!

Like Cayce, Edwards found that he was able to heal just as successfully absently; when the patient was hundreds or even thousands of miles away. He had many spectacular successes, including several with healing cancer. In the final years of his life, Edwards was receiving as many as two thousand letters a day, from people seeking help. If he were still alive I think he might well have done much today to help those suffering from AIDS.

Another British healer of considerable note is George Chapman, of Liverpool, who first became interested in spiritualism through the death of a baby daughter, in 1945. Having an interest in the healing aspects of spiritualism, and then developing some success as a medium, Chapman worked initially with the spirit of a Cree Indian healer. He then became associated with the late eminent eye specialist and surgeon Dr. William Lang.

Lang died in 1937, aged eighty-four. A number of people who knew Lang when he was alive have witnessed Chapman working while channeling Lang. They say the resemblance is uncanny. As Lang takes over, Chapman's face is transfigured. It seems to become wrinkled and many years older. Chapman assumes Lang's characteristically stooped attitude, speaks in Lang's high-pitched, slightly quavery voice, and snaps his fingers imperatively when he needs surgical instruments passed to him, as Lang did.

No true surgical instruments are used, for the surgery is of a spiritual nature. The patient is fully clothed and the medium/doctor works with his hands just above the surface of the physical body, working on the ethereal body. Yet patients speak of having felt (non-painful) sensations of, for example, incisions being sewn up. Throughout the operation, and the whole time he is in trance, Chapman's eyes are tightly closed. He says that afterwards he remembers nothing of what took place, only of Dr. Lang's initial arrival.

The husband of Jean Cull, another greatly respected British medium, found himself introduced to

188 ·~· Doors to Other Worlds

spiritual healing in a very forceful manner. Robert Cull was a tremendous skeptic. On the one hand he watched his wife developing as a medium and totally believed in her and trusted her. Yet on the other he could not accept that it was the spirits of the dead who worked through her. In his case even seeing was not believing. Then one day the spirits turned the tables on him!

At the house of some friends, Jean and Robert had been discussing healing with their hosts and another couple who were present. Robert watched some healing done to help a skin complaint one of the men was suffering from, when the subject of his own allergic rhinitis came up. Reluctantly Robert agreed to let one of the male mediums work on him, and sat down in a wooden chair. When he woke up, some time later, everyone was looking at him in a strange way.

It turned out that he had gone into involuntary trance and, while in that state, had spoken as a Chinese gentleman calling himself Chi. Chi said that he would be Robert's constant companion from then onwards and would work with him, doing spiritual healings! It took a very long time before Robert could even believe that it was himself speaking on the tape recording they played for him, let alone that he had a spirit guide and was to be a healing channel.

Becoming a Healer

The first requirement for you, as a spiritual healer, is good health for yourself. You cannot hope to heal others if you are the one in need of health. To this end you need to follow a good diet, cutting out junk food and things like sugar (the "white death") and bleached flour.

Eat plenty of fruit and vegetables. Acidic fruits, such as the pear, peach, plum, orange and lemon, are especially good for you since they act upon the liver and tend to cleanse the blood.

I don't for one moment suggest you become a vegetarian; however, don't overindulge in red meats. Try to keep a balanced diet — though what is balanced for one may not be for another. Avoid becoming grossly overweight or underweight.

Drink only decaffeinated tea and coffee, and make sure they are naturally decaffeinated, not chemically. The tea I drink is actually caffeine free, rather than decaffeinated. It is called "Kaffree" tea (distributed by Worthington Foods, Inc.) and is made from the leaves of the Rooibus shrub *(Aspalathus linearis),* an African herb. It tastes very much like a pekoe, yet is caffeine free.

Try to develop a mind that is sympathetic and receptive, in an attitude of kind helpfulness. If you feel at all selfish it sets up an immediate barrier to helping others. Work on your mediumship development as I have outlined it throughout this book. It is especially important to get into contact with your spirit guide, since through him or her you will be drawing on the spirits who will help you with healing.

Chakras

The physical body is connected to the etheric or spiritual body at centers known as *chakras.* Part of the development of any psychic and healing ability is to stimulate those chakras by raising what is known as the *kundalini* power; power that travels through the body and generates energy.

The chakras are linked with actual physical glands, and there are seven of them. The first, lumbar (or base) chakra is at the gonads; the second, spine chakra is at the adrenals; the solar plexus at the lyden; the heart at the thymus; throat at the thyroid; third eye at the pineal, and the crown chakra at the pituitary.

Here is what I say about this in my book *Buckland's Complete Book of Witchcraft* (Llewellyn, 1986):

> *In meditation the mysterious psychic energy can be sent up through these centers. This very potent force is called the Kundalini, or "Serpent Power." As this mighty force begins to flow within you, these vital psychic centers — the chakras — begin to open in successive order . . .*

> *As the vital forces begin to flow through the nervous system, the individual achieves a sense of well-being and peace. The subconscious begins to clear itself of the negative and undesired patterns of feelings and images that have been programmed into it through your lifetime. The cosmic force of the Kundalini very naturally operates in a calm, relaxed, contemplative atmosphere. As the succession of opening chakras continues, your awareness and perception of life flows continually from within. A new vibrancy permeates your being.*

Yes, getting the kundalini power to flow through the chakras very definitely sets up a new vibrancy. But how to get that power to flow? The first step is the preparation for meditation, as outlined in Chapter Five. Do your head rolls, deep breathing and relaxation, then awaken the chakras as follows.

Each of these seven centers is associated with a color, going through the spectrum. The base chakra is red, spine is orange, solar plexus is yellow, heart is green, throat is blue, pineal is indigo and crown is violet.

As part of your meditation imagine each of these centers, one at a time, and see it enveloped in its specific color. Concentrate your energies first on the base chakra, and see it enveloped in a swirling ball of red light. Imagine this light ball spinning around, clockwise, getting faster and faster. After a few moments of this, see the ball of light start to move up to the position of the second chakra, at the adrenals. As it moves up see it gradually changing color to orange, so that by the time it gets to that second chakra position it is pure orange. Again have it swirl around and around. Then move it on up to the third chakra, at the solar plexus, changing to pure yellow as it moves. Go on up through all the chakras until all have been vitalized in this fashion. Finish off by changing the color to white and seeing the ball of light grow larger and larger until it envelops your whole body.

It is important that the chakras be awakened in the right order, from base to crown. You will find you feel a sensation of warmth with, perhaps, a faint pricking at each center, as you "awaken the fiery serpent." Always do this before you attempt any spiritual healing.

Chakra Centers

The Human Aura

Baron von Reichenbach, an industrial chemist, in the mid-nineteenth century discovered what he termed *odyle*, or the *odic force*. He showed that it emanated from all objects, but especially from the human body, and could be seen by sensitives. The thoroughness and soundness of his scientific experiments — controlled by Dr. William Gregory, Professor of Chemistry at Edinburgh University — made a great impression on the mind of the public at that time.

In 1911 Dr. Walter J. Kilner of St. Thomas' Hospital, London, published a book called *The Human Atmosphere,* dealing with these same emanations, but referring to it as the *human aura*. Kilner was able to prove its existence by developing a screen that could be used by anyone. This screen made the aura visible and was a solution of dicyanin (a product of coal tar) sealed between two pieces of glass. Today it is possible to buy what are known as "aura goggles" which, when worn, allow anyone to see auras.

Three Layers of Light

The human aura consists of a number of layers of light, as it were, expanding outwards from the physical body. The first of these, which is very dark in color and is generally known as the *etheric double,* extends no more than a half inch or so beyond the body's extremities. Beyond that is the *inner aura,* which extends outwards for two or three inches. Then, beyond that, is the *outer aura,* which has been observed extending out six inches or more before becoming invisible.

The inner aura is the one most commonly seen. Its color(s) can vary depending upon the physical and mental health of the person. The outer aura colors also vary, but are usually of a darker hue and therefore harder to discern.

What is meant by the colors of the aura? There doesn't seem to be a consistent interpretation of the colors seen, for they vary with the individual. In very general terms it can be said that dark colors, especially browns and reds, indicate anger. A greyish-brown shade might mean selfishness; a greenish-brown, jealousy. Red can indicate sensuality and physical

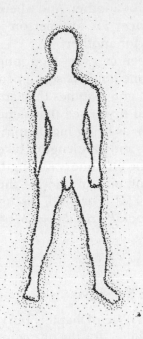

The Aura

love, whereas pink is connected with love on the mental and spiritual planes. Orange is frequently a sign of pride and ambition; yellow shows intellectuality; deep blue-green is sympathy. Light blue is indicative of devotion while dark blue is spirituality and religious feeling. These are as suggested by Charles W. Leadbeater, an Anglican clergyman who became a leading figure in the Theosophical movement.

Many psychics claim that they can see gaps in auras which indicate a physical problem. Others speak of seeing black clouds in areas where there is disease. You need to be very cautious in diagnosing with the aura for, as I have said, the colors seen can vary with the individual. Where brown means one thing for one person it can mean something totally different for another. And where a gap in the aura may mean cancer for one person it could just as easily be indigestion for another!

Not only that but what is seen can vary from one psychic to another. Just because one sensitive sees a person surrounded in a pink cloud, and assumes they are madly in love, don't be surprised if you see that same person in blue, and think of them as being highly spiritual. It all has to do with vibrations and wavelengths. Like a radio, the one psychic might tune into one wavelength of the person while you are tuning into another — she may be on AM while you are on FM! (For a full discussion of color vibrations, see my book *Practical Color Magick*, Llewellyn 1983.)

Train Yourself to be Sensitive

While persevering in psychometry (see Chapter Ten), also cultivate these aura-seeing abilities, for the one complements the other. Try to see and feel the vibrations coming from people you meet, in all walks of life. Look at them against a light background, with the light behind them, and also with dark shadow behind them. You will find that either one or the other is better for you to be able to see their aura. Try to focus in on any emanations issuing from their body. If you are standing or sitting near them, try to sense everything they are giving off unconsciously. Try to pick up on their emotions and on their state of health.

When walking down the street, get into the habit of picking up on people as they pass. Just a brief sense of them will do. What colors do you see? Are they happy or sad? Intense or carefree? Busy or relaxed? You will soon find you are able to pick up certain vibrations from just a casual meeting.

Then go on to "probing" them. How are they, physically? Do they have any health problems? If so, what are they? Practice anywhere and everywhere.

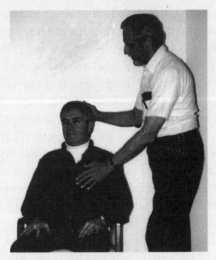

Spiritual Healing

You, the Healer

Now you are ready to try some psychic healing, or at least some diagnosis. You will (hopefully) get to the point where the spirits will be coming through you and they will be doing all the diagnosis and prescribing. But to start with, get an idea yourself of the feel of a patient; an idea of what is probably wrong with her or him.

Your "patient" can be sitting up in a chair or lying down, it doesn't matter which. To start, join hands with her and ask her to match breathing with you. Take some good deep breaths together then settle into a regular, normal breathing pattern. This will help both of you attune to the same wavelength. Now tell your patient to close her eyes and relax.

With your hands about an inch or so off the body, pass them slowly over the patient, in all directions, and see if you sense any physical marks or problems. You will be surprised how easily you pick up on cuts and bruises; even moles and pimples! Be aware of any anomalies in her aura. Don't yet try to interpret their meaning but move your hands to that area and concentrate.

Now close your eyes and mentally call upon your spirit guide to come through. Ask for assistance in diagnosing the patient. Relax and let your hands move wherever you feel they should. Let your mind remain open so that whatever comes into it can come in unopposed.

Say whatever comes into your head. You may well find yourself using words and terms you are unfamiliar with. Have a tape recorder going, or someone taking notes. Afterwards, check out all that you are able. If you know anyone familiar with medical terms — a nurse, doctor, medical assistant, or whomever — ask them to go through the notes or listen to the tape, and explain or confirm what is said (confirm in the sense of acknowledging the correctness of the terms or phraseology).

Do this diagnosis with as many people as you can. It is good if you can work on someone who has already had a medical examination and can therefore afterwards confirm, or otherwise, what you have said. The more you do it, the more the spirits will grow accustomed to working through you.

Distant Healing

Whether or not you are successful at spiritual healing by working on a patient who is physically present, you may well be very successful at absent, or distant, healing. Many successful healers have actually found they have far better results with patients who are far away than they do with those immediately present.

Work as you do for normal spiritual contact, as medium in a séance. Sit and prepare yourself. Move on to contact with your guide. Now have someone read out the name and address of the person seeking healing. Ask for contact with that person, and for a diagnosis to be made. Relax and let come what may, making note of what you say, hear or see. Having made your diagnosis, now ask what would be the best treatment, and again make note of what you receive. Ask your guide for healing energies to go to that person.

At this stage in your progress, do not attempt to pass on your received prescriptions for cure. Have the patient go through normal medical channels, so that you can verify all that you have learned through spirit. You will be amazed how accurate you will find the Second Level medical experts to be! And you will know when the time is right to pass on all that you receive.

If you have no success, no matter how long and how hard you try, don't feel rejected. Not everyone is meant to be a spiritual healer. It may mean that your talents as a medium between this level and the next lie in another direction. Or it may simply mean that the time is not yet right for you to enter into the field of healing.

As with so much in mediumship, perseverance is the keyword. Keep practicing; especially keep working on communicating with your guide.

XVII

DEVELOPMENT CIRCLES

Lack of Good Mediums

Looking back over the relatively short history of spiritualism, it seems there was a vast number of mediums from the late 1800s well into the twentieth century, but in the years since the Second World War there has been a very definite decline. Today it seems difficult, if not impossible, to find a medium; good, bad, or indifferent. Why is this? There are several reasons. The most cogent, I feel, is due to the advancement of home entertainment.

Spiritualism was born in the mid-nineteenth century. It is not surprising that there then came a sudden blossoming of mediums, as more and more people became aware of the possibility of spiritual contact and of the latent talents they themselves possessed. As I said in earlier chapters, we all have these "powers" within us. It is simply a matter of realizing we have them, and then drawing them out. Many were able to draw them out, and many became very accomplished as intermediaries between this world and the next. We must also admit that many more were not so accomplished — or were too lazy to develop themselves — but found the various phenomena of spiritualism easy to duplicate in a fraudulent manner (more on this in Chapter Twenty).

With the doorway to the next world cracked open, whole groups of people joined together to communicate with those they had known and loved and who had passed on to the next level of existence. Groups would get together — "Home Circles" — meeting on a regular basis to help each other develop and to bring out the abilities of mediumship in one another. These Circles of enthusiasts were the core of the spiritualist movement.

But then came the invention of radio and, later, of television. By then the novelty of communication with the world of spirit had worn off. It experienced an upsurge — quite a sizable one — throughout the periods of the two World Wars. At those times people felt the need to contact loved ones killed in the conflicts, but afterwards the necessity was not there, or not so immediate, for most people.

With vast numbers of the population wooed away from spiritualism by the magic of radio and television, plus the advent of talking pictures, women in the work force, time and money for a wide variety of recreation, the number of Home Circles — and thereby the number of developing mediums — declined until it became almost non-existent. The number of spiritualist devotées shrank to minute proportions, and it is no wonder. Yet spiritualism did not die out.

New Wave of Psychics

At first glance it might seem that the modern education received by the younger generation would sound the death knell on such a practice, and religion, as spiritualism. Yet the reverse is true. Previously children have slavishly followed the religion and beliefs of their parents, and their grandparents before them, without question.

There was such a thing as family tradition. But today, children are taught to think for themselves. No longer do they automatically become Roman Catholics, Jews, Episcopalians, or whatever. No longer do they mouth the beliefs and arguments of their elders, parrot-fashion. Today they are far more capable of making up their own minds and don't hesitate to do so. And in doing so there is a tendency to reject many of the traditional values.

I think it is a bad thing to reject anything out of hand. But I think it is a good thing to give serious thought to what you have been told and to reach your own decision on whether or not it is believable. Perhaps not surprisingly, this has led to a swing back to interest in spirit communication, among other things.

Many people are becoming jaded with television. They are bored with the endless repetition of inane situation comedies and police dramas. People are now looking for alternatives to being couch potatoes.

Astrologers will say that it is the dawning of the Age of Aquarius that is responsible, and so it may be. But whatever the reason, there is today a far greater awareness of other realities, of psychic senses and sensibilities, of alternate paths of religious belief and expression. Rather than mediums, we are finding a veritable plethora of "psychics" who read tarot cards, palms, runes, crystal balls; who chart horoscopes, do healing with a wide variety of methods, and even use talking boards and tip tables. The psychic has replaced the medium in many ways.

Full Circle

Life goes in circles, or cycles. Nowhere is this more noticeable, perhaps, than in the field of fashion. What was "in" ten years ago suddenly makes a comeback. Short skirts for women, wide ties for men; double-breasted suits; hairstyles. But it is not only fashions. Interests, fads, whole lifestyles, all seem to come and go in huge circles. And interest in spiritualism is but another example.

As part of the "New Age" — a misnomer, since the vast majority of the practices that are put under this unsatisfactory heading are ancient ones — we have seen the advent of channeling on a grand scale. I will look more closely at this phenomenon in the next chapter; for now suffice it to say that it is akin to mediumship and, indeed, has been a stepping stone in the journey back to Home Circles.

Sir Arthur Conan Doyle

Channeling was quite a fad, with well-known personalities getting involved with it, just as in earlier days well-known personalities got involved in spiritualism (Sir Arthur Conan Doyle, author of the Sherlock Homes stories, for example). One of the positive things about channeling was that it did remind many people of the phenomenon of mediumship. Consequently Spiritualist churches have seen an increase in membership. Home Circles have started up again.

In England the Home Circles never did die out as completely as they seemed to here in the United States. Even today there are still development groups meeting, throughout Britain, who have been doing so for years. But even so there was a noticeable decline and now, also, the Circles are once again on the increase there.

Your Own Development Circle

It would seem, then, that this is an ideal time to establish more Home Development Circles for mediumship. Actually this is already happening. Small institutes and metaphysical bookstores have never stopped giving classes, lectures and workshops on various aspects of spiritualism, clairvoyance, psychometry, table tipping, healing, etc. But now these classes and workshops are also being held in people's homes. Groups of friends are getting together, just as they did in "the old days," to investigate and experiment with these forever fascinating subjects.

If you have a strong interest, whether as a potential medium or just from the curiosity point of view, why not form a development circle of your own?

A Home Circle should be made up of six to ten people; twelve at the most. All should be dedicated to the point of committing themselves to attending every meeting, unless there are truly exceptional circumstances. Meetings should be held once a week. The actual day is not important but it should be on the same day every week, at the same time and in the same place. It is possible to meet at a different house each time, on a rotating basis, but far better if you can keep to one house and even one particular room, for you will find there will be quite a build-up of vibrations over the months.

New people should not be introduced haphazardly. The idea is for the members to grow completely comfortable with one another, to develop together, and also for the spirits to be able to attune and develop with them. Any new person coming into the established Circle tends to throw everyone "out of sync," as it were. This is not to say that you may never bring in others, just that it should not be done on a whim. No more should "visitors" be invited, for they, too, will interfere with the harmonious atmosphere that has been generated.

So you need a group of people who, from the start, know that they must be responsible and dedicated. You can expect to work together for a very long time. Most established Circles have been going for years.

Appoint a leader. He or she should be the most experienced and/or most well read. The leader is responsible for everyone and responsible for recognizing where talent is showing itself, so that it can be especially encouraged. All should be supported in their development, with no one ignored.

Everyone should be encouraged to read as much as they possibly can on all aspects of spiritual contact and psychic development (see Bibliography). Time should be taken at the start of every meeting to discuss what has been read and learned and for people to ask questions of one another.

There is no need to work in darkness; however, a low light setting does seem to help development in its earlier stages. Later on you can come back to full light if you wish. As I mentioned in Chapter Eleven, it is a good idea to have fresh flowers in the room. Make sure the telephone is disconnected and that there are going to be no interruptions.

Start by everyone going through the relaxation and breathing exercises, then join in together with a little singing. Again as mentioned in Chapter Eleven, the song should be light and happy. Now take a moment to relax and make yourselves comfortable. Feet flat on the floor, legs uncrossed. Take hands in a circle and, if you wish (this is not mandatory), join together in a short prayer. Then let the leader make a statement of purpose.

This will initially be to the effect that you are all there to make contact with the spirit world and to develop yourselves as mediums. The leader will ask for help and guidance from the spirit guides in all you undertake and will emphasize your dedication to the work before you.

In the first weeks of meeting you might concentrate on psychometry, clairvoyance and clairaudience, developing much as I have indicated in this book. Do readings for one another; get the feel of letting things come through. As I've said before, no matter how strange something sounds to you, it may have great significance to another. Don't try to interpret; just relay what you receive. In these early weeks everyone should be encouraged to participate.

Into Mediumship

When the leader feels that all are comfortable with one another, that the initial shyness of speaking out has passed, then you should start concentrating on one person at a time. Here is one good reason for not having too many people in your Circle. With a smaller number you will be able to work with everyone having some development time each week. With a large number you wouldn't have the time to fit in everybody. Later on, certainly — some months down the path — you will get to the point where you will only concentrate on one person each meeting, but in the early days it is nice if everyone has an opportunity to try their hand.

So, take the first person for concentrated development and let the leader stand behind that person while they and everyone else joins hands to form a circle. The leader should hold his hands out over the head of the medium, concentrating energies into her, or him. Everyone should try to send positive energies to the medium, around the chain of hands, as the leader asks the medium's guide to come through.

At this point it may be that the medium gets some direct connection with her guide, or with a spirit. She should speak out with whatever comes through. It is unlikely, at this stage, that any physical phenomena will be experienced, though it certainly has been known to happen. More likely the medium will see or hear her guide, or the spirit, and will relay what is seen or heard. If such contact is made, you may progress much as I described in the chapter on the talking board, with the leader acting as spokesperson and asking questions.

If nothing comes through, don't be discouraged. Don't let the medium feel ineffective. All the energies there are important. Not everyone will develop as a good medium; this should be understood from the start. Also, some will be more attuned to working at, say, psychometry while others excel at clairaudience, for example. But everybody's energy is useful in the Circle. Like the cells of a huge battery, you are all contributing to the energy of whoever is working on their progress at the moment.

After a Circle you should feel refreshed and energized. You should not feel depleted in any way. If you find yourself exhausted on a regular basis, then leave that Circle. Energy should flow freely from you, and flow freely to you from spirit. If your energy is being sapped, leaving you the worse for it, then you need to make a break. This is not to say that there is anything "evil" happening in such a group. It is just that some individuals do strongly draw other people's energy to themselves. They do this quite unconsciously, but they can adversely affect others. If you happen to be one of those who is being sapped by such a person (you won't necessarily be able to tell who it is), then it is better to leave rather than spend all your time feeding them.

Record Keeping Is Important

It is most important that you keep accurate notes of all that takes place in the Circle. Only in this way can you see the progress you are making. Run a tape recorder and have someone taking notes. These days some groups even have a video camera going, just in case there are any physical manifestations. You can probably keep just one tape for this, since it can be used over and over when there is nothing of any importance in the session. Keep only what is worthwhile on video. But it is good to keep the audio tapes in their entirety and to build up a library of them, showing how the Development Circle has progressed over the months and years.

If you keep at it, you will get to the stage where you have two or three really good mediums in your Circle and where you can enjoy regular communication with the Second Level.

Rescue Circles

Once established, some Circles like to spend time on what they term "rescue work." It seems there are a large number of spirits who do not realize that they have died. They wander about, literally haunting their old neighborhoods, wondering what has happened to them.

Should you, or your Circle, come into contact with such a spirit, take time to explain to him (or her) where he is. (Such spirits are often contacted by way of the Ouija board.) Tell him that he is preventing his own progress by attaching himself to an area he can never return to. Tell him to go forward into the light.

Those people who are accomplished at astral projection, and can decide where they want to travel, frequently go out searching for these "lost spirits" in order to help them cross over to the Second Level.

Let your Circle always be on the lookout for those spirits who seem confused and uncertain as to where they are or what has happened. Ask your guide(s) to direct any such lost ones to you and to your Circle.

XVIII

CHANNELING

Channeling vs. Mediumship

A common question seems to be, "What is the difference between channeling and spiritual mediumship?" In some ways they are very much alike, insofar as the channeler is acting as a medium for non-physical entities to come through to this plane. But nonetheless, there are some distinct differences.

First of all, the majority of channelers are acting as direct voice conduits for the personalities they access. Very, very few engage in clairvoyance, clairaudience or similar activities, but seem to be strictly direct voice. Secondly, the personalities they transmit are not always the spirits of those who have previously lived on this physical plane. This is not the case with all channels, admittedly, but certainly with a large number. Thirdly, there is usually only one personality who is channeled on a regular basis. And, as an extension of this, the personality comes through and, in effect, lectures or preaches to the audience; some have very definite directives they wish to impart. There is not the introduction of a variety of spirits, as in mediumship.

In spiritual mediumship, as we have seen, the medium is acting as a channel for the spirit of a recently deceased loved one to return to this level and reconnect with those left behind. Primarily there are exchanges of a personal nature, with reference to family matters. In channeling, it is as though the audience is attending a lecture by a visiting dignitary who has a general message to deliver. There may well be a chance for questions at the end of the lecture but these are usually limited to one or two questions only — not necessarily of a personal nature — by whomever manages to get recognized.

Origins

It is not always easy to establish the origin of a channeled entity. Some claim to have last been alive on this planet at the time of Atlantis, or of Ancient Egypt. Others say they have never lived in this physical plane at all. Some say they are from a far distant planet in another galaxy.

Jane Roberts' "Seth" said he was "individual portions of energy, materialized within physical existence." Elizabeth Clare Prophet channels what she describes as "ascended masters" — spiritually advanced beings who no longer live on the physical plane. Judy "Zebra" Knight (born Judith Darlene Hampton) claims that her "Ramtha" once lived thirty-five thousand years ago on the now lost continent of Lemuria, or Mu. Jessica Lansing's "Michael" says he is "of the mid-causal plane" — made up of a thousand fragments of an entity like itself. Jach Pursel's "Lazaris" says that he has never been in human form; he is a "group form" living in another dimension. Darryl Anka's "Bashar" says that he is from the planet Essassani, five hundred light years away. Elwood Babbitt has had Jesus speak through him, or so the entity claims.

These are perhaps typical of channeled entities and are some of the better known ones. One thing they have in common is that they all are, or claim to be, more highly evolved than we poor mortals and are here to help us advance. Another interesting point — and one that I don't think has ever been addressed — is that, regardless of the sex of the channel, virtually all the entities manifest as males.

Channeled Material

Most of the material that is channeled boils down to the same general teachings. We are taught that the universe is a multidimensional, living being; that we create our own reality, and that love conquers all.

As Jon Klimo says, in *Channeling* (1987):

> *Virtually all of the sources above the lower astral levels tell us that from their vantage points they know the entire universe to be a living spiritual being of which each is a living part. According to Universal Law, we are evolving through a series of embodied and disembodied lives toward an eventual reunion with the one God, which is the underlying identity of All That Is. In the meantime, we maintain an ongoing condition of identity with this God, though we are unaware of it. It is by virtue of the higher Self that we are connected to this deeper truth.*

Some few channeled entities have been "doom and gloom" prophets; notably the egotistical and strangely materialistic "Ramtha." They have warned of impending disaster, urging that we get our act together and hurry up and save the world. Still others have urged their followers to give away all their worldly goods, stockpile food and water, and wait for Armageddon!

What should you believe? Whom can you trust? The answer, as with any spiritualist medium, is to study and judge the quality of what is being received and then to make up your own mind. Don't be *told* what to do. Listen to the advice and decide *if it is right for you.*

Most of the lectures that come through channelers are good and positive. If you find that the channel you are listening to on a regular basis is other than positive, you might want to question a little more. An entity from another galaxy (for example) might well be more advanced in many ways, but that doesn't necessarily mean that he is in the best position to tell you what to do with your life savings, your home, or your family. Don't sell your real estate; don't give up your job; don't leave your spouse and family, just because a channeled entity says you should. Think it through. Question the source. And research the background of the channeler.

Again to quote Jon Klimo:

> We must guard against the charisma of authority . . . just because we may believe that information comes from some glamorous paranormal source, we should not fail to scrutinize its content and weigh our response to it as carefully as if it came from a more pedestrian source . . .

How to Channel

Many of the established channels started spontaneously. My wife, Tara, and I were once talking with Jach Pursel, who channels "Lazaris." Jach said that he had been in the insurance business, living in Florida. He had no great interest in matters metaphysical and certainly knew nothing of channeling. His wife, of that time, Peny, did introduce him to meditation, since he was working long hours and finding himself in need of a good relaxation technique. One day he did his meditation and, so far as he knew, fell asleep during it. Jach said that when he woke up Peny was sitting looking at him in amazement. Apparently Lazaris had come through and started talking. The voice was completely different from Jach's — a most distinctive voice, at that time heavily accented. The voice also had different speech patterns from Jach's. Peny had the presence of mind to write down what was said. When they found that this same thing was happening every time Jach tried to meditate, they started using a tape recorder. Jach just couldn't believe it when he heard the voice!

Many other channels have had similar initiations. So it is possible that you can start channeling at just about any time, if the entity to come through decides that the time is right! But if you don't want to just sit and wait and hope, then there are steps you can take.

Start out as with all your spiritualist and psychic development exercises. Do your deep breathing, relaxation, and go into your meditation. *Don't forget to set up that barrier of blue or white* (or whatever color you prefer) *light about you.* Set a tape recorder to record; then give out to the universe that you are ready and open to channel; you are willing to accept and direct any intelligence that should wish to come to you. You can make this statement silently within, if you so wish, but I feel it probably has more impact (on your own conscious and subconscious, apart from anywhere else) if you make it aloud. Just say, in effect, "I hereby give permission for any positive force to speak through me. I am ready and willing to channel information for the education and for the good of all concerned." Then sit quietly and wait.

Several channels speak of mentally "falling away" from themselves as they give themselves over to the channeled force. To achieve this kind of sensation, after making your statement mentally take yourself on the start of the meditation journey you did in Chapter Seven. Take yourself to where you start moving down the steep path, descending to the lower level. But keep going down. Imagine a cave, a tunnel or an opening of some sort into the earth. Go into it and find more steps, a ladder, or something similar, whereby you can descend further and further.

You may well find that when you go down you do not reach the bottom, for the channeling takes over before you do. Some established channels say that they are climbing down a ladder and then, before they know it, they are falling off the ladder, backwards, into a deep sleep.

Next thing you may know is that you are waking up again. But if you do reach the bottom, see yourself in a large cavern, or small earth home, or something of that nature, and simply sit down quietly to wait. If, after sufficient time (about twenty minutes, I'd suggest), nothing has happened, then start the return journey. Try again another day.

Don't forget that not everyone is a channel. Not everyone will get results. Try no more than about twenty minutes at a time. Try once, twice or three times a week, over several weeks. Be prepared for a long wait. You may be lucky and receive contact in a short time, but it may take long weeks of perseverance.

Real or Imagined? Channeled or Inspirational?

A lot of what is presented as channeled material is probably no more than the vocalized unconscious mind of the channeler. The person is not consciously pretending to be a foreign entity but is unconsciously presenting material from their own mind "packaged," as it were, as if coming from a separate source.

This has been described as *inspirational speaking*. The channel might never be able to speak so well, to be so eloquent, in everyday life. But he or she, speaking as a "channeled entity," is able to bring out material that he didn't even know he had access to.

How do you, the listener, judge this material? The same way you judge all other channeled material — ask yourself "Does it make sense?" "Does it apply to me?" "Will it work, in a positive way, to advance my life?" If the answers to all of these are "Yes," then it really doesn't matter what is the true source of the material you are hearing.

As Lazaris puts it:

> *First, are the teachings limited? Are the teachings giving you the sense that you are less than you are? Second, can I apply this? Can I use this? What's it going to do for me? Third, as I apply what's being said, am I happier? Am I more myself and is my life working better? Fourth, when I come away from the experience, am I feeling and am I thinking more positively?*

XIX

DEVELOPMENT EXERCISES

Throughout this book I have spoken of developing your abilities in the various aspects of mediumship. In everything I have talked about, *practice* is the keyword. I therefore now offer a few exercises that you can work on, that will aid you in your development.

One thing to remember: don't overdo things. Don't try to do something — be it scrying (crystal-gazing), clairvoyance, psychometry, or whatever — and keep trying till you are blue in the face! Apart from getting discouraged, you will rapidly terminate your interest in that, and perhaps in the whole field, and you will drag down your psychic defenses to the point where you could suffer both physically and emotionally. But by taking small bites on a regular basis you will progress, gain in strength, and much sooner reach fruition.

At the root of all psychic development is good breathing. In *Amazing Secrets Of the Psychic World,* which I co-authored with Hereward Carrington, I spoke of the life-giving property of fresh air and the fact that by simply breathing fully, it contributes to your living fully. Some exercises we gave were:

1. Stand before an open window, or out of doors, free from all restrictive clothing. Exhale forcibly, bending the body forwards and relaxing the muscles. Then stand up straight and place both hands over

the abdomen. Now breathe as deeply as possible against those hands, expanding the abdomen as much as possible without allowing the chest or ribs to expand in the least. Again, exhale forcibly.

2. After five or six such breaths, place your hands on either side against your ribs. Now breathe in deeply, pressing out the ribs but without allowing either the abdomen or the upper chest to expand.

3. After five or six breaths as before, place your hands on the upper chest, just below the neck, and breathe with this portion of the lungs, without allowing either the ribs or the abdomen to expand.

You will find that it's not easy to so control your breathing. After you have mastered it, though, you can go on to the *complete breath:*

4. Take a number of good, deep breaths, starting with expanding the abdomen then the ribs and then the upper chest, one after the other in the one breath. Try to control this intake in the three stages, one after the other. Then as you become more accomplished merge them, one into the next, so that you have something akin to a rolling motion as the breath moves up the body. Breathe in through the nose and out through either the nose or the mouth.

From there go on to establishing a mental image of the breath, as you breathe it, in the form of light. See it coming into the body and filling it. As you breathe out, see the light forcing out all the negativity, in the form of dark colors (black, dark browns, blues, greens and reds). You can see the light entering from wherever seems most comfortable to you: through the third eye, into the heart, up through the feet . . . whichever you prefer. Just be consistent and always see it entering at the same place.

For the exit of the negativity, see that being driven out of all bodily orifices, one after the other, and end with it leaving through all the pores of the skin. End with the whole body — every little extremity — completely filled with fresh, vibrant, positive light.

Trance Development and Chakra Enhancement

Analyze your "falling asleep" pattern. Try to catch yourself at just the point of falling asleep and to "hold on to yourself," as it were, as long as possible in that state until you can hold no more and you actually do fall asleep. This is excellent practice so that you will always be in control of yourself, no matter how deep the trance you enter.

In Chapter Sixteen you learned how to awaken the chakras by moving swirling light up your body. The English medium, Ivy Northage, suggests that you might also imagine each chakra center as a flower and see it opening up. Eastern philosophy links the centers with the "thousand petaled lotus," but you can see the chakras as any flower you wish. A different flower at each center, if you would like, though please be consistent and always have that same one at the same center.

As the light swirls about it, see the petals slowly open and fold back until the whole bloom is there. If you can tie in a psychic smell of the flower at that point, that would be wonderful. Then move that colored light on up towards the next chakra.

Raising Your Vibrations

As I've mentioned previously, we are all vibrations. Everything is made up of vibrating matter; be it a tree, a rock, a blade of grass or a human being. We are all vibrating matter. The world of spirit is vibrating at a different rate from the physical world, so if we can raise our vibration rate sufficiently it will facilitate our communication with the Second Level.

A worthwhile suggestion is given by Jon Klimo (*Channeling*) for raising your vibrations. Imagine a dial, with an attached knob, fastened to yourself. See it calibrated from one to ten. The dial is to indicate the raising of your consciousness vibrations.

In your meditative state, start to turn the knob and see the needle on the dial move up from zero to one. Feel, sense, and know that your vibrations are moving up towards the ideal of being on a completely spiritual level; where you are at one with your Higher Self. Slowly turn the knob on up to two, then three. Take your time with this. Adjust your senses with each turn of the knob.

It may take a number of sittings before you feel able to get as high as ten and be at one with your Higher Self. Don't rush this; take it a little at a time. As you raise your vibrations, also feel your emotions being cleansed.

Self-Induced Trance

A popular way of going into trance involves gazing at a candle flame. Try this as an exercise. You may find that it works better for you than the gradual relaxation technique. It is basically a variation on the method of gazing at a bright object that I described in Chapter Eight.

You can be sitting or lying down. Soft music playing in the background may or may not help . . . some people are simply distracted by the music. Have a lit candle at eye level or below. Any other light in the room should be low.

Gaze steadily at the candle flame. Take a number of slow, deep breaths and start to give yourself suggestions of relaxation. Such suggestions as: "I am feeling completely comfortable and at peace. I am totally relaxed. As I look into this candle flame my eyelids become heavier and heavier and want to close."

You will find that your eyelids do indeed become heavier and want to close. Let them close. And when they do, continue with the suggestions that you are comfortable and secure. Go on to say that you are drifting down deeper and deeper into relaxation and into a state of trance.

From there you can go on to meet with your guide or contact the spirits. For some people the candle flame is more effective than any other method. Try it and see if it is for you.

Billets and Billet Reading

Billet reading is sometimes done by mediums on public platforms and by Spiritualist ministers in Spiritualist churches. *Billet* is the French word for a letter. In the spiritualist sense it is a written note, usually on a piece of paper about the size of a playing card.

Sometimes the person is asked to just write a name on the piece of paper — the name of the deceased, perhaps — and sometimes they are asked to write a question. The paper is then folded up and collected. The medium will go on to name the name (and, perhaps, contact the spirit of the person named) or answer the question. This is done without the medium opening the folded billet.

Billet reading is a development of psychometry, for you are picking up the feelings of the person from the paper. You will find that by practicing your psychometry it will not be difficult to pick up the writing on a small piece of paper, even if it is folded up. A good exercise, for practice, is to take a number of pieces of paper, all the same size. On each one write a different letter of the alphabet. Fold the paper in half, then in half again. Place the folded pieces of paper in a hat, basket or other container, and thoroughly mix them up.

Take out one billet at a time, hold it and concentrate on it, and try to pick up in your mind what letter is written on it. When you have decided (I will not say "guessed" because you should not be guessing; you are picking it up by psychometry), open the paper and see if you are correct. Record your answers and see how many you get right.

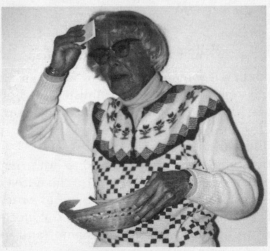

Billet Reading

You can proceed from there with names written on the pieces of paper. Write the names of different people whom you know to be in spirit. Again, fold them and mix them. If you have someone to work with, have them write down the names. Working in a group or Development Circle, each write a name and then pass the billets around so that each has one to work with.

The last step, of course, is to work with questions. Have someone write short questions and see if you can pick up what is written and then answer the question. Again, in a group each write a question, fold the papers and distribute them.

Flower Reading

Some mediums — Chris Meredith of San Diego, is an example — do flower readings. The sitters each bring a flower and place it in the center of the Circle. It can be any sort of flower, though if there happen to be more than one of a type (two red roses, for example) then you will need to tie on a piece of thread, or something similar, to tell one from the other.

The medium should not know who has brought which flower but will take them up one at a time and concentrate on them. He or she will be able to say who brought the particular flower and, through it, reach that person's spirit contact.

You can practice this in your Circle by each person bringing a flower and, after they have been placed together and mixed, each drawing a flower.

Look for other exercises you can do to hone your skills as a medium. There are many, and there are certainly variations on the ones I have given. Remember, practice makes perfect.

XX

◇◇◇◇◇◇◇◇◇◇◇◇◇◇◇◇◇◇◇◇◇◇◇◇◇◇◇◇◇◇

SPIRITUALIST FRAUD

Easy to Fake

Spiritualist mediumship is easy to fake. But just because it is easy to fake does not mean that all mediums are fraudulent. Far from it. Yet this is a conclusion to which many seem all too ready to jump. Professional conjurers especially seem to make this elementary mistake. They see, or hear of, a medium levitating a table (for example) and just because they know how they could fake such a thing they immediately assume that must be the only way to do it, and therefore that the medium also must be faking it.

It would be possible to place a home movie projector in a cabinet and rear-project film onto a screen so that the whole thing outwardly looked like a working television set. Yet what you actually would have is far from being a television set; it would be working in a totally different way. This is a good analogy for the workings of a conjurer, or a fake medium, compared to a true medium. The end product may seem the same but it really isn't at all alike; the mechanics are completely different. Yet, as I have said, the conjurer invariably assumes that his way of doing things must be the only way.

Frauds In All Walks of Life

But having said that, I would be the first to admit that there are fraudulent spiritualist mediums . . . just as there are fraudulent cops, fraudulent bank managers, fraudulent salespeople, and frauds in all walks of life. And yes, there is a very high percentage of fraud in spiritualism.

Why is this? It is because mediumship is a very easy thing to fake. And it's also because there are many, many people who are grieving over the death of a loved one and are therefore in an extremely vulnerable position when it comes to the possibility of communicating with that lost spirit. Fake mediums who take advantage of such bereaved people are probably the most contemptible swindlers of all.

In his book *The Psychic Mafia*, Lamar Keene, a repentant, formerly fraudulent medium/minister, describes how he rose to fame and, especially, fortune in Florida. There he was operating a Spiritualist church where all the mediumship was of the fraudulent variety. Keene and a fellow conspirator kept a complete filing system on all the regular members of their congregation, plus others who came sporadically. All the details concerning these people, their lives and the lives of those near and dear to them who had died, were carefully filed and cross-indexed. The purpose, of course, was so that these facts could be presented by the "medium" minister at opportune moments to impress the recipient.

This was a common practice with many such frauds nationwide and was not confined to one church in one area. Many (though obviously not all) Spiritualist churches operate with outright fraudulence. Lamar Keene, in his book, includes photographs of dozens of information notebooks kept by such "mediums." In fact there was even a network for exchanging information, for working on the not inconsiderable number of people

who travel around the country visiting mediums and
Spiritualist churches in different areas, always hoping to
make contact with a deceased relative or friend.

Keene says:

> *The code used by mediums in their files is simple.*
> *Some of the common conventions are: A cross beside*
> *a name means the individual is dead; a circle, that*
> *he's alive. A heart next to a name indicates someone*
> *with who (sic) the sitter is or once was in love.*
> *"G.G." next to "Blue Star" would mean that a*
> *medium had assigned the sitter a girl spirit guide*
> *named Blue Star.*

Some of the big spiritualist camps have been almost
totally fraudulent in what they have presented to the
people who attended sittings there. Camp Silver Belle, in
Ephrata, Pennsylvania, and Camp Chesterfield, in Indi-
ana, in particular were caught out and thoroughly
exposed, according to Keene. Camp Silver Belle, before
the exposé, took in up to a million dollars a year from
the thousands of believers who flocked there, hoping to
sit with the camp's famous mediums.

The blatancy of some "mediums" is incredible.
Again to quote Keene:

> *How did I get information? Simple. I became an*
> *expert pickpocket. It was even easier than that, most*
> *of the time, when all that was required was for*
> *Raoul (his confederate) or me — depending on*
> *which of us was conducting the séance — to lift a*
> *woman's purse — in the total darkness while she*
> *was occupied listening to spirit voices from the trum-*
> *pet — take it into another room, and go through it.*
> *Later the purse was returned to the same spot, and*

when the séance concluded and the lights came on, the woman suspected nothing.

This method yielded not only social security numbers and other confidential data, but also many of the personal objects which the spirits later returned as "apports."

The unscrupulous ministers would also remove small objects from pockets and purses and file them away. The sitter might well miss the object, though perhaps not for a few days or even weeks, and might subsequently ask the spirits for help in finding it. It was then doubly effective for the object to be "apported" into the séance room or church many weeks later!

Tricks Of the Trade: Billets

One of the most popular forms of spiritual reading done in the church setting is using billets (see Chapter Nineteen). The premise is that by the sitter writing the name(s) of the deceased on the paper and/or asking a question, it is easier for the medium/minister to make contact with the spirit on the Second Level. In a manner similar to psychometry, the billet makes the connecting link. In reality, of course, it can also provide a fake "medium" with a certain amount of information to start off with — if he can somehow get to read it.

The sitter writes on the billet, signs it, and it is then either folded up a couple of times or it is placed, unfolded, into an envelope and sealed. A basket is passed through the congregation and the billets are dropped in. This basket is then taken up to the front of the church and placed beside the minister.

There are now several ways for the medium to handle the billets. He or she might simply hold the folded paper in his hand, or between his hands, concentrating on it, and then start to speak. Or he may lay the paper on the Bible in front of him. One effective way I have seen is for the "medium" to take up the billet, hold it for a moment, and then to light it from a burning candle nearby and drop the burning paper into a receptacle. As it burns, he identifies the writer and goes into making contact with the spirit(s). This is, as I say, very effective, for how could he possibly read what he has just destroyed?

The answer is that he has not actually destroyed the whole thing! Sometimes — and especially if this type of cheating is to be done — the pads of paper given out for billets are made up of sheets with nice little decorations, or Biblical quotations, printed around all four edges. Consequently the sitter is forced to write his or her name or question in the center section of the sheet. The instructions given are that the sheet should then be folded in half and in half again. Ostensibly this makes it impossible for anyone to be able to read what is written on it. However, when the "medium" picks the folded paper out of the basket, he holds it by the corner which is the center of the folds and surreptiously tears off that section. The rest of the billet is quite visible in his fingers and looks as though it is still whole. It is this which is lit and dropped into the receptacle. Meanwhile the minister, with his hand below the level of the pulpit, has only to tuck his thumb into the palmed center piece, and it opens up so that he can read what is written there!

A billet switch and the one-ahead method is another way of doing things. The minister has a blank billet (let's call it "A") palmed in his hand. He takes up a folded billet ("B") from the pile and unobtrusively switches the two. He can then hold the visible ("A") billet up to his forehead or wherever he likes, as though concentrating on it. Meanwhile he is looking down at his other hand, out of sight, which is flipping open the written billet ("B") so that he can read it. At the end of the reading he openly drops the (blank) billet ("A") into the receptacle and takes up the next one ("C") from the basket. He can now use "B" in the same way he used the blank, switch them and read the new one ("C") while holding up "B." And so on. Outwardly he is picking up a billet from the basket, holding it up in plain sight while he "reads" it, then putting it down and doing the same with the next. Very effective.

Another method is used when the billet is placed, unfolded, in a sealed envelope. The envelope is simply laid down for a few moments on top of the Bible. But the Bible is a fake, being hollowed out with a light inside it. Unseen by the congregation — since the top of the pulpit or rostrum slopes back — the light is switched on and the minister can read what is written, through the envelope.

Another variation on this, not requiring a fake Bible, is for the minister to wipe some lighter fluid over the face of the envelope. This will momentarily make it transparent, so that the billet can be read through it. The fluid will quickly evaporate so that even if the writer wants the billet envelope back, it will show no signs of tampering.

Materializations and Trumpets

In darkness many things are possible. Even with the usual low wattage red bulb alight, it is not possible for sitters to detect accomplices who are dressed all in black. If the medium works from inside a cabinet, he or she may also be dressed in black and come out to help make things happen.

It has been said that ectoplasm (see Chapter Fifteen) looks a little like gauze or chiffon. In many cases it *is* gauze or chiffon! In a totally dark séance — and most physical mediums call for total darkness to facilitate materialization — it is easy for someone dressed all in black to slip on a simple covering of chiffon, or something similar, and be dimly seen by the sitters as a materialized spirit. The main problem, for the medium, is how to get the material into the séance room.

Lamar Keene speaks of stuffing material into his undershorts. One female "medium" he talks about did it even more effectively. She was not in the least perturbed if investigators wanted to search her beforehand. In fact she welcomed it, for she had carefully folded a sheet of chiffon and packed it into a condom, which she then inserted in her vagina!

Some permanent séance rooms (especially at the fraudulent camps) are set up with hidden doors, so that accomplices can slip into the room under cover of darkness and move objects, appear as materializations, whisper in people's ears, or whatever else is called for.

Martha Lomax, a "medium" caught in the Camp Chesterfield scandal, was a very large woman. At her séances three diminutive "spirits" would materialize and flit about the room, sometimes even climbing into the laps of the sitters. They were, in fact, Lomax's three small children, who entered through a trapdoor, under cover of the darkness.

Movement of the trumpet can similarly be accomplished by black-clad "mediums" and/or assistants. The trumpet usually has a band of luminous paint around its bell and mouthpiece, so that its movement can be seen by the sitters in the dim red light. Sometimes a trumpet will actually have secret extra length which can be pulled out of it to extend it beyond the luminous bands — without the sitters' knowledge, of course. This means that the "medium" can manipulate the trumpet from a distance and make it fly about the room and rise up to the ceiling.

The trumpet is usually very light in weight. Another way to move it is for the "medium" to slip what normally looks like a pen out of his pocket. It is actually a telescoping rod, much like the pointers that can be purchased for lecturers to point at maps, etc. Extending the rod, the "medium" can then cause the lightweight trumpet to move even while sitting some distance away from it.

To have voices come from the trumpet is simply to have the "medium," or accomplice, in black, speak through it as it "hovers" close to the sitter. Lamar Keene had an interesting variation on this. The sitter would be able to take hold of the trumpet and would actually feel the slight vibrations in it as the voice spoke. Keene did this by using a second, unpainted, trumpet. Speaking through this second one, in the dark, pointed at and close to the one being held, caused the slight vibrations in the one being held. He got the second trumpet into the séance room by using a piece of cardboard rolled around his leg and tucked into his sock. Pulling it out in the dark, Keene would then roll it into a cone shape and thus had his second trumpet!

Levitating Tables and Banging Tambourines

With the above it obviously behooves the sitter to be very wary at séances held in complete darkness (or with no more than a red bulb alight). Happily few of these types of séances are held these days. Most reputable mediums will operate in full light, or at most with slightly dimmed lighting.

However, even in better lit rooms it is possible for fraudulent "mediums" to operate. Take the levitating of a table, for example. After some tipping, and rotating up onto two or even one leg, it may well happen that the table finally lifts all four legs off the floor.

One way a fake "medium" can accomplish this is by having a short length of wood or metal attached to the forearm (one or both arms) and to slip this under the edge of the table at the same time that their hands are placed on the top surface of the table. In an emergency they can slip an ordinary dinner knife, or even a fork, into their sleeve to do the job; putting the handle under the watch strap is one way of holding it firmly. With this projection under the table — if it is a light one, such as a card table — it is easy to lift the table into the air. Everyone present would swear that there was no way it could be faked!

Another way is to have a nail driven into the table top, with just the smallest amount of its head still projecting. By the "medium" slipping the ring she is wearing (such as a wedding band) under the head of the nail as she places her hands on the table top, a purchase can be gained enough to give a lift to the table.

Sometimes a medium will sit inside the cabinet with tambourines, bells and/or musical instruments on a small table beside her. She is tied into the chair, so that there is no way she can even touch the things on the

Fraudulent Table Tipping

table. Yet when the curtain is drawn across, and she has gone into trance, the sitters hear the tambourine being banged, the bell rung and all the other sounds. At the end of the séance the medium is found still securely tied in the chair.

Some of the fakers are simply good at getting out of, and back into, knotted rope. But others are sneakier. They will use a chair with an arm, or arms, that can be detached. The sitters may tie the "medium" into the chair and tie the knots as tightly as possible. But when the curtain is drawn across all the "medium" has to do is press a button, or twist the arm, or in some way cause the upper arm of the chair to come free so that the medium can use her still-bound hand quite freely. At the end she simply slips the chair arm back to click into place and the rope and knots remain untouched.

Gathering Information

If you should go to a séance, church meeting or spiritualist demonstration where you are asked to write out a question, and given a clipboard on which to write . . . beware! There are a variety of fake clipboards available through professional conjurers' supply houses that look absolutely like the genuine article. You can write on a piece of paper resting on the clipboard, then tear off the paper and keep it, yet the damage has been done; the clipboard itself now has a copy of what you wrote. The clipboard can then be taken backstage before the start of the sitting or demonstration and the accumulated information transferred to the "medium." The fact that you have kept the piece of paper on which you wrote has no bearing on it. Usually the clipboard has a cleverly hidden sheet of carbon paper and second sheet of paper, to pick up all that is written. No matter how slim and "normal" the clipboard may look, it can be such a fake.

Lamar Keene speaks of two-way mirrors and even of a sophisticated electronic listening device. This he used from a house across the street from his church, so that he could pick up information from the congregation as they stood talking before going into the service!

AFTERWORD

Yes, there has been — and probably still is — a lot of fraudulence in spiritualism. But I repeat, that doesn't mean that it is all fraudulent. There have been and still are many good, sincere mediums. In the early days D. D. Home was outstanding, as was Leonora Piper. In more recent times Gladys Leonard, Winifred Coombe Tennant, Geraldine Cummins, Eileen Garrett, Ena Twigg and Estelle Roberts were excellent. George Anderson is an outstanding present-day medium. Anne Gehman is another, as is Shirley Calkins Smith, Jean Cull, Pamela White, Cheryl Williams, Douglas Johnson and many more. There are many good, dedicated spiritualists out there, if you just take the time to track them down. And remember to judge each of them on an individual basis. Examine what they say. Make up your own mind whether or not you should accept it.

Know that mediumship is not necessarily a special gift. I strongly believe that we all have the capability within us to make contact; to bridge the gap between this level and the next. I hope that this book will help bring out that specialness in each of you, so that there will be less need for the frauds and so that all can see that death is not the end. There is a life beyond, and we will see our loved ones again.

Raymond Buckland

APPENDIX

FRAUDULENT MEDIUMS ACT
OF 1951

In Great Britain prior to 1951, if anyone was caught swindling using spiritualism, fortunetelling, or the like, the only way they could be prosecuted was under the old Witchcraft Act. This seemed rather silly in the middle of the twentieth century, so the Witchcraft Act was repealed and it was replaced by the Fraudulent Mediums Act.

The Fraudulent Mediums Act, 22nd June, 1951

An Act to repeal the Witchcraft Act, 1735, and to make, in substitution for certain provisions of section four of the Vagrancy Act, 1824, express provision for the punishment of persons who fraudulently purport to act as spiritualistic mediums or to exercise powers of telepathy, clairvoyance or similar powers.

Be it enacted by the King's most Excellent Majesty, by and with the advice and consent of the Lords Spiritual and Temporal, and Commons, in this present Parliament assembled, and by the authority of the same, as follows:

I. (1) Subject to the provisions of this section, any person who:

    (a) with intent to deceive purports to act as a spiritualistic medium or to exercise any powers of telepathy, clairvoyance or other similar powers, or,

    (b) in purporting to act as spiritualistic medium or to exercise such powers as aforesaid, uses any fraudulent device, shall be guilty of an offence.

(2) A person shall not be convicted of an offence under the foregoing subsection unless it is proved that he acted for reward; and for the purpose of this section a person shall be deemed to act for reward if any money is paid, or other valuable item given, in respect of what he does, whether to him or to any other person.

(3) A person guilty of an offence under this section shall be liable on summary conviction to a fine not exceeding fifty pounds or to imprisonment for a term not exceeding four months or to both such fine and such imprisonment, or on conviction on indictment to a fine not exceeding five hundred pounds or to imprisonment for a term not exceeding two years or to both such fine and such imprisonment.

(4) No proceedings for an offence under this section shall be brought in England or Wales except by or with the consent of the Director of Public Prosecutions.

(5) Nothing in subsection (1) of this section shall apply to anything done solely for the purpose of entertainment.

II. The following enactments are hereby repealed, that is to say :

     (a) the Witchcraft Act, 1735, so far as still in force, and

     (b) section four of the Vagrancy Act, 1824, so far as it extends to persons purporting to act as spiritualistic mediums or to exercise any powers of telepathy, clairvoyance or other similar powers, or to persons who, purporting so to act or to exercise such powers, use fraudulent devices.

III. (1) This Act may be cited as the Fraudulent Mediums Act, 1951.

     (2) This Act shall not extend to Northern Ireland.

∾·✺·✺·✺

The Constitution of the United States of America does not contain anything similar to the British Fraudulent Mediums Act. However, there are various state and local laws which do cover the legality of so-called fortunetelling and mediumship.

BIBLIOGRAPHY

This bibliography includes those books mentioned in the text plus others which I feel may be of help or of interest to you.

Abbott, David P. *Behind the Scenes With the Medium*. Open Court, Chicago 1907.

Atkinson, W. *Mind-Power*. Progress, Chicago 1908.

Bach, Marcus. *Miracles Do Happen*. Waymark Books, New York 1968.

Bagnall, O. *The Origin and Properties Of the Human Aura*. Routledge and Kegan Paul, London 1957.

Barbanell, Maurice. *This is Spiritualism*. Jenkins, London 1959.

Bardens, D. *Ghosts and Hauntings*. Taplinger, New York 1968.

Bayley, H. *The Lost Language Of Symbolism*. London 1951

Bentine, Michael. *Doors of the Mind*. Granada, London 1984.

_____ *The Door Marked Summer*. Granada, London 1981.

Bernstein, M. *The Search For Bridey Murphy*. (New Edition) Doubleday, New York 1965.

Besterman, T. *Crystal-Gazing*. Rider, London 1924.

Blundson, Norman. *A Popular Dictionary of Spiritualism*. Arco, London 1961.

Boddington, Harry. *The University of Spiritualism.* Spiritualist Press, London 1947.

Bradley, D. B. and R. A. *Psychic Phenomena.* Parker, New York 1967.

Britten, Mrs. Emma Hardinge. *Autobiography.* London.

Brown, Slater. *The Heyday of Spiritualism.* Hawthorn, New York 1970.

Buckland, Raymond, and Carrington, Hereward. *Amazing Secrets of the Psychic World.* Parker, New York 1975.

Buckland, Raymond. *A Pocket Guide to the Supernatural.* Ace Books, New York 1969.

————. *Anatomy of the Occult.* Weiser, New York 1977.

————. *Buckland's Complete Book of Witchcraft.* Llewellyn, St. Paul 1986.

————. *Practical Color Magick.* Llewellyn, St. Paul 1983.

————. *Secrets of Gypsy Fortunetelling.* Llewellyn, St. Paul 1988.

Butler, Willam E. *How to Develop Clairvoyance.* Weiser, New York 1971.

————. *How to Develop Psychometry.* Weiser, New York 1971.

————. *How to Read the Aura.* Weiser, New York 1971.

Carrington, Hereward. *Your Psychic Powers and How to Develop Them.* Dodd Mead, New York 1920.

————. *The Physical Phenomena of Spiritualism.* American Universities, New York 1920.

Christopher, Milburne. *Mediums, Mystics and the Occult.* Crowell, New York 1975.

Circlot, J. E. *A Dictionary of Symbols.* Philosophical Library, New York 1962.

Cook, Mrs. Cecil. *How I Discovered My Mediumship.* Lormar, Chicago 1919.

Crinita, Joey. *The Medium Touch.* Donning, Virginia Beach 1982.

Crookall, R. *The Study and Practice of Astral Projection.* Aquarian, London 1960.

Cull, Robert. *More to Life than This.* Pan, London 1987.

Davis, Andrew Jackson. *The Principles of Nature.* New York 1847.

_____. *Death and the After Life.* New York 1865.

Dingwall, Eric, and Langdon-Davies, John. *The Unknown: Is It Nearer?* Signet, New York 1968.

Doyle, Sir Arthur Conan. *The Edge of the Unknown.* Putnam's, New York 1930.

_____. *The History of Spiritualism.* Doran, New York 1926.

Ebon, Martin, editor. *True Experiences in Communicating with the Dead.* New American Library, New York 1968.

Edmonds, John W. *Spiritualism.* New York 1853.

Edmunds, Simeon. *Spiritualism: A Critical Survey.* Aquarian, Hertfordshire 1966.

Edwards, Harry. *The Evidence for Spirit Healing.* London 1952.

_____. *The Healing Intelligence.* Taplinger, New York 1971.

_____. *The Mediumship of Jack Webber.* London 1946.

_____. *The Science of Spirit Healing.* London 1945.

Eisenbud, Jule. *The World of Ted Serios.* Morrow, New York 1967.

Feilding, Everard. *Sittings with Eusapia Palladino.* University Books, New York 1963.

Flammarion, C. *Mysterious Psychic Forces.* Unwin, London 1907.

Fodor, Nandor. *Between Two Worlds*. Parker, New York
1964.

———. *Encyclopedia of Psychic Science*. London 1934.

Ford, Arthur, and Bro, Margueritte H. *Nothing So Strange*.
Harper and Row, New York 1958.

Ford, Arthur. *The Life Beyond Death*. Berkley, New York
1971.

———. *Unknown But Known*. Harper and Row, New York
1968.

Fortune, Dion. *Psychic Self-Defense*. Aquarian, London
1967.

Garfield, Laeh M., and Grant, Jack. *Companions in Spirit*.
Celestial Arts, Berkeley 1984.

Garrett, Eileen J. *Many Voices*. Putnam's, New York 1968.

———. *The Sense and Nonsense of Prophesy*. Creative Age,
New York 1950.

Gauld, A. *The Founders of Psychical Research*. Shocken
Books, 1968.

Guiley, Rosemary. *Harper's Encyclopedia of Mystical and
Paranormal Experience*. Harper, San Francisco
1991.

Hall, Manley P. *Solving Psychic Problems*. Philosophical
Research, Los Angeles 1956.

Hardinge, Emma. *Moderm American Spiritualism*.
University Books, New York 1970.

Hill, Douglas, and Williams, P. *The Supernatural*.
Hawthorn, New York 1966.

Hogshire, Jim. *Life After Death*. Globe, Boca Raton 1991.

Hollen, H. *Clairaudient Transmission*. Keats, Hollywood
1931.

Holzer, Hans. *Born Again*. Doubleday, New York 1970.

———. *Ghosts I've Met.* Ace Books, New York 1965.

———. *Psychic Photography.* New York.

Hunt, Stocker. *Ouija, the Most Dangerous Game.* Harper and Row, New York 1985.

Hyslop, James. *Life After Death.* New York 1918.

———. *Contact with the Other World.* New York 1919.

Jones, Lloyd K. *Development of Mediumship.* Lormar, Chicago 1919.

Kardec, Allan. *The Book of Mediums.* Weiser, York Beach 1970.

———. *The Spirits' Book.* Amapse Society, Mexico 1857.

Keene, M. Lamar. *The Psychic Mafia.* St. Martin's, New York 1976.

Khei, F. R. C. *A Brief Course in Mediumship.* Health Research, Mokelumne 1965.

Kilner, Walter J. *The Human Aura.* (Original Title: *The Human Atmosphere*) University Books, New York 1965.

Klimo, Jon. *Channeling.* Tarcher, Los Angeles 1987.

Knight, Marcus. *Spiritualism, Reincarnation and Immortality.* Duckworth, London 1950.

Kübler-Ross, Elisabeth. *On Death and Dying.* Macmillan, New York 1969.

Leonard, John C. *The Higher Spiritualism.* Philosophical Book Co., Washington, D.C. 1927.

Litvag, I. *Singer in the Shadows.* Macmillan, New York 1972.

Martin, Joel, and Romanowski, Patricia. *We Don't Die.* (Medium George Anderson) Putnam's, New York 1988.

———. *We Are Not Forgotten.* Putnam's, New York 1988.

Meek, George W. *After We Die, What Then?* Ariel, Columbus 1987.

Melville, J. *Crystal Gazing.* Weiser, New York 1970.

Monroe, Robert A. *Journeys Out of the Body.* Doubleday, New York 1971.

Montgomery, Ruth. *A Gift of Prophecy.* Morrow, New York.

_____. *A World Beyond.* Fawcett, New York 1971.

Moody, Raymond. *Life After Life.* Bantam, New York 1976.

_____. *Coming Back.* Bantam Books, New York 1991.

Moses, William Stainton. *Direct Spirit Writing.* London 1878.

_____. *Higher Aspects of Spiritualism.* London 1880.

_____. *Spirit Teachings.* London 1883.

Mühl, Anita M. *Automatic Writing.* Steinkopff, Dresden 1930.

Nelson, Robert. *Secret Methods of Private Readers!* Nelson, Columbus 1964.

Northgate, Ivy. *Mediumship Made Easy.* Psychic Press, London, 1986.

Overlee, Vernon W. *The Psychic.* Mora, Canaan 1983.

Pearsall, Ronald. *The Table-Rappers.* St. Martin's, New York 1972.

Pebbles, J. M. *The General Principles and the Standard Teachings of Spiritualism.* Health Research, Mokelumne 1969.

Pike, James A. *The Other Side.* Doubleday, New York 1968.

Podmore, Frank. *Mediums of the Nineteenth Century.* University Books, New York 1963.

Pollack, J. *Croiset the Clairvoyant.* Doubleday, New York 1964.

Price, Harry. *The Most Haunted House in England.*
London 1940.

Prince, W. *The Case of Patience Worth.* University Books,
New York 1964.

Proskauer, Julien J. *Spook Crooks.* Burt, New York 1932.

Regardie, Israel. *The Art of True Healing.* Helios,
London 1964

Reilly, S. W. *Table-Lifting Methods Used by Fake Mediums.*
Ireland Magic, Chicago 1957.

Robert, K. *The Seventh Sense.* Doubleday, New York.

Roberts, Estelle. *Fifty Years a Medium.* Corgi Books,
London 1969.

Shepard, Leslie A., editor. *Encyclopedia of Occultism and
Parapsychology.* Avon, New York 1978.

Sherman, Harold. *You Can Communicate with the Unseen
World.* Fawcett, New York 1974.

Smith, Alson J. *Immortality, the Scientific Evidence.* Prentice
Hall, New Jersey 1954.

Spence, Lewis. *Encyclopedia of the Occult.* London 1920.

Spraggett, Allen. *The Unexplained.* New American
Library, New York 1967.

Stearn, Jess. *Edgar Cayce, The Sleeping Prophet.* Doubleday,
New York 1967.

_____. *The Search for the Girl with the Blue Eyes.* Doubleday,
New York 1968.

Theobald, Morell. *Spirit Workers in the Home Circle.* Unwin,
London 1888.

Turner, Gordon. *An Outline of Spirtual Healing.* London
1963.

Tuttle, Hudson. *The Arcana of Spiritualism.* Two Worlds,
Manchester 1921.

Verner, Alex. *Practical Psychometry*. British Psychological Institute, 1935.

————. *Table Rapping and Automatic Writing*. Fowler, London.

Wallis, E. W. and M. H. *A Guide to Mediumship*. Health Research, Mokelumne 1968.

Wavell, S. *Trance*. Dutton, London 1967.

White, Stewart E. *The Unobstructed Universe*. Dutton, New York 1952.

Wilde, Stuart. *Affirmations*. White Dove, Taos 1987.

Xavier, F., and Vieira, W. *The World of Spirit*. Philosophical Library, New York 1966.

Zolar. *Zolar's Book of the Spirits*. Prentice Hall, New York 1987.

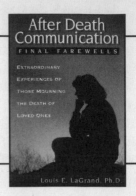

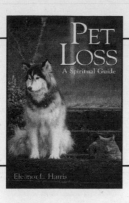

Pet Loss
A Spiritual Guide
ELEANOR L. HARRIS

The grief that follows the death of a pet has only recently been recognized and treated by the mental health community. While it is absolutely normal and healthy to mourn, the grieving process can be crippling emotionally, mentally and even physically. Here is the first book to examine how to cope with this unique loss from a broad, spiritual perspective. It addresses the emotional responses of the grieving process, the pros and cons of euthanasia, and the logistics of making final arrangements for your pet's body. You will learn the psychological facts about the human-animal bond; how to deal with the initial shock of your loss, as well as your anger, guilt and sadness; and the truth about what happens at the cemetery or crematorium. Various religious beliefs are presented, with a focus on pagan funeral rituals and meditations.

1-56718-347-6
304 pp., 5 3/16 x 8, illus., softcover   **$9.95**